Holiness through Faith.

LIGHT ON THE WAY OF HOLINESS.

BY R. P. S.

AUTHOR OF "THE SECRET OF VICTORY," "THY MAKER IS THY HUSBAND," "IS THE VII. OF ROMANS TO BE THE CONTINUED EXPERIENCE OF THE CHRISTIAN?" "THROUGH DEATH TO LIFE," ETC., ETC.

"PURIFYING THEIR HEARTS BY FAITH."
Acts xv. 9.

REVISED EDITION.

NEW YORK:
ANSON D. F. RANDOLPH & CO.,
770 BROADWAY, COR. OF 9TH STREET.

These pages, written in America from week to week for a periodical, were collected by an English publisher and issued in book-form. They are now printed—with the Author's revision—for circulation in his native country.

THE PUBLISHER.

PREFACE.

"THE faith which was once delivered to the saints" was a faith which made them victorious over the world, the flesh, and the devil. By it Enoch walked with God three hundred years, having before his translation this testimony, "*that he pleased God.*" And yet God has "provided some better"—not an inferior—"thing for us" in this dispensation, which is noontide glory as compared with the twilight of revelation to the infancy of our race. The danger of the hour has been in occupying men's souls, not too much, but too exclusively, with their standing in Christ, while the standard of walk which should accompany it has been deemed as impracticable. Our privileges form the measure of our responsibility. The reception of the free and full remission of sins through Him "who his own self bare our sins in his own body on the tree," is incomplete, unless the expressed purpose of that sin-bearing be also accepted: "that we being dead to sins should live unto righteousness." Christ in mercy "gave himself for us," but it was in order "that he might redeem us from all iniquity."

A work of faith allows of no apology, and requires but little explanation. Written with the simple and earnest desire to remove prejudice from honest hearts, and to lead fellow-believers into a perfect soul-union with Jesus, these papers are not intended to enter upon the range of systematic theology. As to their essential truth, I have proved it in my own experience, as have also many witnesses around me, and I do not shrink from the solemn responsibility before God of pressing the truth, which forms their subject, upon Christians everywhere. And yet, since every transmission of God's light is refracted by the medium through which it passes, I should not be surprised if advancing light should modify these statements upon some details and interpretations of passages, not affecting the essential truthfulness of the views here urged. We are not infallible. While enlightened, we are not inspired. While it is God's own light, His glorious light, in which we walk, yet we are not yet able to gaze upon all its fullness. May our spiritual vision be made clear, by a full deliverance from sinning, to behold the glory of God in the face of Jesus Christ!

In the words of another, "There is within me an inward testimony to the truth, so deep that all the world cannot shake it. It is the work of God upon my heart. Who will dare limit the power of God? Who will say that God, whose love is infinite as it is free, cannot give such proofs of love as He pleases to His creatures? Has He not the right to love me as He does? Yes, He loves me, and His love is *infinite.* I do not doubt it. And He loves you too, dear M——, in the same manner. This is eternal love manifested,—the heart of God drawn out, expressed towards his creature.

"In this state we understand the mutual secrets of the Lover and the beloved. Who will so deny the truth of the Lord as to question this? When I hold my Beloved in my arms, in vain does any one assert, 'It is not so; you are deceived.' I smile inwardly and say, '*My Beloved is mine and I am His.*' If we receive the witness of men, how much greater is the witness of God!"

CONTENTS.

ILLUSTRATIVE INCIDENTS.

The circumstances narrated as illustrations in this work have all come under the Author's own personal experience or observation, and are given with the conviction of their literal truth in every particular.

HOLINESS THROUGH FAITH.

CHAPTER I.

INTRODUCTORY.

BELOVED READER, — Do you feel that your expectations at conversion have been practically realized as to the righteousness, peace, and joy, in the Holy Ghost, which you then read were the characteristics of the kingdom? Is there not some terrible deficiency in your experience, for which you are unable wholly to account? Did you not expect to be kept more perfectly than results have realized, and had you not the warrant of the Word for this? When you compare your own inward experience with others who, like yourself, it may be, have lived prayerfully, and in earnest devotedness of outward effort to God, do you not find the same sad and God-dishonoring story of unsanctified affections and wandering desires: a divided heart, with, it may be, outward failure in temper, or otherwise; things that have, with fearful certainty, been the index of remaining inward corruption? Would you be willing, when you are leading a sinner to Christ, for him to see all that remains in your own heart of unbelief?

When some certain form of sin, known to your own soul, is presented to you, although you turn from it, is there not a response down deep in the soul, that contradicts the verdict that you have given, and which says of the evil thing, in unmistakable tones, "I LOVE IT!" Ah! there is the fatal thing —you *love it* after all. Now what a man *loves*, in a certain sense, that man himself *is* in character. His affections show the central powers of his being. Out of the same fountain come sweet waters and bitter, and upon the same tree grow grapes and thorns.

Leaving for the present the question whether those who claim to have received Holiness through Faith are in the right way, would it not be the greatest blessing of your life, beyond all earthly gifts, if there were some means of your receiving and grasping the rest of soul, the full victory over sin, and the hourly communion with the Lord, which these claim to have received by faith? As a young minister said lately to the writer, "I would give all the world to believe and feel as you do,—I would give up my property, my prospects, my all!" While he could not trust our way of faith, he saw that the end set forth contained blessings immeasurably beyond what he had, or expected to have, in this life, and blessings that the Word seemed in many passages to set before him.

So far, my brother, we agree together. We greatly long that you and we might "walk by the same rule, and mind the same thing," "having the same mind, being of one accord, of one mind." How much else is there also that we agree in perfectly; that we were ruined, hopeless, helpless sinners, going down to hell, when God, in his wondrous mercy, quickened us by his Spirit to see our lost condition, and then led us to the cross, to behold Jesus bearing "our sins in his own body on the tree." We together know that, being born of God, we received, in addition to the old nature (the flesh) a new nature, an actual existence begotten of God, of "incorruptible seed;" and that, believing in Jesus, we have eternal life. Together we have turned to God from our old idols, "to serve the living and true God ; and to wait for his Son from heaven," as our hourly expectation. Together we are begotten "unto a lively hope by the resurrection of Jesus Christ from the dead." It may be that together we have learned from the same pages by the same Spirit, to come out from the world and be separate—refusing the well-watered plains of Sodom, in order to dwell on the mount with faithful Abraham, possessing nothing —as to the spirit of our lives—but a tent for our pilgrimage, and an altar for our sacrifice. We have both, perhaps, in this path, parted with much or most that men hold dear, as to ease or reputation. And lastly, we both with equal honesty of purpose, I trust, desire to know the whole of God's blessed truth, and knowing it, to walk in it.

In all this we have long been and are now with you. During many long years of earnest service for God, we were also with you in the disheartening life of bondage, which you confess, to inward corruption ; the old or natural man continually brought us "into captivity to the law of sin, which was in our members." We verily looked for a progressive, partial deliverance and were sometimes cheered by the temporary withering of some particular branches of the corrupt tree ; but after long years, we found it still vigorous, and sending forth fresh shoots.

We have gone a step farther, and it may be with you, in that, in public, in private, and in print, we opposed a teaching which we verily believed to be a lowering of God's standard of holiness, joined to spiritual pride. Being blind to the light, we denied the evidence of those who had sight, and who said that the sun shone. We did not understand that what was claimed was not "absolute perfection," but that *up to the measure of to-day's consciousness* they were kept by faith, and that all the glory was given to Christ equally and in the same way with that of remission of sins. Like yourself, we were stumbled—just as sinners are by false professors—by seeing the counterfeits of this life in Christ. We did not remember that from an angel of light, down to the smallest things, Satan's plan always is to counterfeit God's work and truth ; and that wherever there was a counterfeit, there we were to look for a divine truth, carefully distinguishing between them.

Dear brother, in how many things have we

agreed together! And now may I in the fear of God tell you how that, while thus one with you, I have been compelled to go farther, step by step, in much prayer, and with much close searching of the divine word. Follow me prayerfully, for I write in calm confidence that God will guide you and me if we are willing, as little children, to be led by the Spirit.

LIGHT ON JUSTIFICATION AND SANCTIFICATION.

First, however, permit me to relate two simple incidents. Soon after my own conversion I sat down beside a dear relative, an earnest man, and a student of the Scriptures, to show him justification by faith, from the Word. We turned to passage after passage that were, to my own soul, as luminous as day. After going through them all, his reply was, "Well, by thus picking out passages here and there through the Bible, you can make up what looks like a doctrine of justification by faith alone and without works, but take the whole of the Scriptures together, and they never meant any such doctrine." When he became a Christian himself, he found justification by faith alone, in letters of light, from cover to cover of the Bible! A few months since I urged upon another dear friend, a most devoted Christian, the principle of sanctification by faith, and not by works or effort; and he gave a similar reply, verily believing that the whole thing was misapprehension of Scripture and spiritual pride. Later, it pleased God to give him a sight of his inward corruption and deep need, and to show him how he could by faith enter into the glorious liberty of those who know the full practical power of resurrection life in their souls, and to lead him into it by the Holy Ghost. The doctrine of sanctification by faith, an immediate work, now shines for him in letters of light upon every page, as it were, of Scripture; and he finds that in living this life of sanctification he is, for the first time, really sitting humbly at the feet of Jesus. His real life of presumption and self-confidence, he now sees, was lived by him while he refused sanctification by faith alone; and that instead of being a testimony to self, as he formerly supposed, the way of holiness is a testimony to the power of the blood of Jesus. He no longer depends partly on himself or his progress in knowledge, but in a direct way only on Christ, and finds what it is to be indeed "redeemed from all iniquity," pure in heart, and "filled with the Spirit."

We could multiply instances, did space permit, among the most instructed, earnest, and devoted Christians whom we know; for it is to the earnest and devout and not to the careless, that God shows this divine secret. These will illustrate the *possibility* of your seeing the whole subject at some future time in a wholly different light.

Dear brother, with such a practical experience of inward failure as you frankly confess to, and with the testimony within your hearing of numbers who have for years walked in the same path with yourself of outward devotedness, and confessed inward failure, are you willing to believe that there may be *some* way of victory provided by grace,—even if ours be not it,—that you have not yet found out: some way of becoming actually "dead to sins," and "living unto righteousness"?

We both would, of course, say in advance that, if there be such a way, it must present these characteristics:

1. It must be a way taught in the Bible.

2. It must be a way in Christ.

3. It must be a way hid from mere intellect,

and revealed by the Spirit to the soul hungering for righteousness.

4. It must exalt the atonement of our Lord.

5. It must make the soul victorious over inward as well as outward sin.

6. It is the fulfilling of the Law of this dispensation.

7. In exalting Christ, it must humble the believer.

Should you find a way with these characteristics, would you be willing to lay aside your preconceived notions, and receive with meekness this word of grace and power? Do you shrink from Jesus taking full possession of your soul, turning out all the money-changers, and making it a holy temple for the Lord? Since your privileges as a believer are no less than those of Paul, are you willing to receive such a power from on high as would enable you to say, "I am crucified with Christ; nevertheless I live; yet not I, but Christ liveth in me;"—"To me to live is Christ;"—"Ye are witnesses, and God also, how holily, justly, and unblameably, we behaved ourselves among you that believe."

"The perfect way is hard to flesh;
It is not hard to love;
If thou wert sick for want of God,
How swiftly wouldst thou move!"

I trust that you will allow me the privilege of again addressing you on this important subject, and meanwhile remain yours in the loving fellowship of the gospel.

CHAPTER II.

A WAY TAUGHT IN THE BIBLE.

IF the way we are seeking to set forth is indeed God's highway of holiness, it will bear the most scrutinizing tests, and it will by them be only made more clear to the heart that is tender before the Lord, not contending for a preconceived system of doctrine, but crying to God to show,—whithersoever it may lead,—His own truth.

As before remarked, it will have several evangelical characteristics, in which, if it fail, both you and I, who hold so much of God's blessed truth in common, would unite in condemning it. First of all, I would ask you to come " to the law and to the testimony," and let us both seek to clear our minds of prejudice, so that, guided by the Spirit in the Word, we may be able to follow where it leads. As indicated in my last, the Scripture seems to me to have the doctrine and the life I have received upon every page, as it were ; but I will try to divest myself, if possible, of my own views while I write, that we may together look straight to the written Word.

Let us read together Paul's prayer in the Holy Ghost for the disciples, and for us among them: "Unto him that is able to do exceeding abundantly above all that we ask or think, according to the power that worketh in us." If we give rein to our yearnings, asking of God whatsoever things we desire, what would be our first instinctive cry? That we might be holy, and pure, and conformed to the image of Jesus Christ. How often has this been our prayer! But not being with faith, or the yielding of the soul fully to Jesus, it was not answered, nor indeed could be. Does not our Lord's gentle rebuke come to our souls: "O ye of little faith, WHY REASON YE among yourselves?" Was it by reasoning or by faith that we thought it impossible to "awake to righteousness, and *sin not*;" "*perfecting* holiness in the fear of God," and serving the Lord "*acceptably*, with reverence and godly fear?"

Faith is above circumstances, surroundings, impossibilities, and above the devil himself; and when we look away from these *directly to God*, who can limit His grace and power? Nay, my brother, when we have made our largest requests of God, He is still "able to do exceeding abundantly above all that we ask or think." I must freely own that this is my continuous experience. Day by day, as I walk in this way of faith and holiness, wonder and praise fill my heart for heavenly communion, inward purity, victory over the world, abounding peace, and the known presence of Jesus in my soul,—blessings that rise above my asking or even my largest thoughts.

We have together passed through the third of Romans, and have had our souls to ring with joy, as we found joined in the same sentence, "All have sinned, and come short of the glory of God," with, "Being justified freely by his grace through the redemption that is in Christ Jesus; whom God hath set forth to be a propitiation through faith in his blood:"—the complete ruin by works, and the complete justification by faith, together in one brief sentence. But, beloved brother, are we under any less obligation to receive, in the sixth chapter, in their plain and obvious import, the words, "How shall we that are dead to sin live any longer therein? . . . . We are buried with Him by baptism into death; that LIKE AS Christ was raised from the dead by the glory of the Father EVEN so we also should walk in newness of life."

I exhaust my utmost powers of memory and imagination to conceive how, as a constant student of the Word, I could ever have understood God to mean in this passage anything else than complete victory over sin, by realized resurrection-life ; for now the continuing in sin seems that monstrous thing of which the soul exclaims in holy horror, "How shall we that are dead to sin live any longer therein?" "Our old man is crucified with Him, that the body of sin might be destroyed, that henceforth we should not serve sin." I know how to pervert such expressions, for I have often, to my own shame and loss, turned the edge of the Spirit's sword by the poor "tricks of the intellect."

But, my brother, let us now be honest with this passage. When are we not to serve sin? Plainly *now.* From what is this deduced? From the fact of the body of sin being destroyed ("rendered inert, or ineffective, as in suspended life," might be the more exact translation). When destroyed? Plainly, previously to our not serving sin. When was the old man crucified with Christ? Evidently, previously to the destruction of the body of sin. "The way of holiness," death unto sin and life unto righteousness, fairly flash in letters of light through such passages. God give you eyes to see them!

We have together looked forward to the purity of heaven as among its chief joys; we have seen, as it were, the priestly hand of Jesus extended in blessing over "the pure in heart," as they that "shall see God." Reading the possibilities of this life by the light of our own experience, rather than by that of the Word, we long looked for real purity of heart as a privilege reserved for another scene of existence. One of the most earnest laborers in the Lord's vineyard in these parts said to me lately, "If, when I preach, the sinners round me saw the remaining corruption of my own soul, the uncontrollable evil thoughts, the self-worship, and the frequent coldness of my heart, they would not listen to me. My heart is a cage of unclean birds!" I have no reason to believe this dear brother to be worse than many others. I have regarded him as devoted and faithful beyond most; but he walked in the searching light of the Word of God, and like Job he abhorred himself, yet without having gone in faith to Jesus for the remedy.

I own with shame that, had earthly eyes seen me through and through, as God saw me,—even while regarded by some as almost a Nazarite in separation from the world,—I could not have preached even among those who loved me best. When the light of the Word shines clearly and steadily into the caverns of the heart, it shows many a revolting reptile and loathsome insect, not discernible in the darkness, or even in the twilight! May God keep us from shrinking from the piercing light of his own heart-searching truth, for its reception is the first step towards "purifying our hearts by faith."

I remember the time when I first saw with clearness the claims of God on me, as one of his children, for purity of heart. I often read of "them that call on the Lord out of a pure heart;" and that the "end of the commandment is charity out of a pure heart, and of a good conscience, and of faith unfeigned, *from which some having swerved*, have turned aside into vain jangling." I often read of "pure minds," "a pure conscience," and that I was to be "found of Him in peace, without spot and blameless." Then I looked within. Oh!

the agony of my soul as I remembered that I was a child of God, and that this inward purity was what God plainly looked for in His children. His command, "As He which hath called you is holy, so be ye holy in all manner of conversation," did for a time seem to me "grievous." I quailed in spirit as I reflected on what a fearful upturning of my whole nature, what terrible conflicts, what rendings of my soul, must come, before the unclean spirits should be wholly cast out. All my past, even my outward devotedness and inward effort, were seen to be so tainted with self and sin that "there remained no strength in me; for my vigor was turned into corruption, and I retained no strength." Then, in my despair, my eye rested on the words "purifying their hearts by faith." How my soul leaped at these words, as in a moment I saw the possibility of my deliverance "*by faith.*" "If then," I exclaimed, "it is by faith, I will trust Jesus for a pure heart, and *now!*" and with the act of faith there distilled into my heart, like the gentle dew, the sweet consciousness of the cleansing blood and presence of Jesus;—"Christ formed in me" taking full possession of my soul, so that with my whole heart I could sing—

"Now to be Thine, yea, Thine *alone*,
O Lamb of God, I come!"

I know not how to describe it in my own words, but I know that "*this* is the victory that overcometh the world, even our faith;" and since then to me to live has been Christ in a different sense and power than I had ever known before. Obedience,—full-hearted obedience,—became then, and is now, the easy yoke that my Lord promised.

An inward realization of purified affections, a blessing exceeding abundant above all that I had been able to ask or to think, has made obedience simple and natural; so that I can receive that word, "Seeing ye have purified your souls in obeying the truth, *through the Spirit*, unto unfeigned love of the brethren, see that ye love one another with *a pure heart* fervently." Thus has come a harmony into my existence,—a *re-adjustment* of the whole nature, spirit, soul, and body, to Christ,—that must be the wonderful reality of the words, "Christ formed in you," "Christ in you," the being "filled with the Spirit," the "not I, but Christ liveth in me,"—and, "the life which I now live in the flesh, I live by the faith of the Son of God."

Temptation comes to me more fiercely than

ever before, at times for days together; but temptation is not sin, for my Lord was tempted. There is, moreover, now this difference—that temptation finds me within my armor, and behind the shield of faith, so that it is my privilege to quench—not some—but ALL the fiery darts of the wicked one. It seems as though temptation is now from without, rather than from my own heart, and the struggle not so much a wrestling "with flesh and blood," as against wicked spirits,—a contest for my position of being seated by faith with Christ in the heavenly places,—the Canaanite rather than the wilderness enemies. There is much land yet to be possessed, but trusting thus in Jesus, the song of victory precedes the contest, and day by day is known the power of those words, "Grow in *grace*, and in the knowledge of our Lord and Saviour Jesus Christ," and of all that "*He* is able to do."

Does this seem presumption, my brother? I would ask your *heart*,—not your system of doctrine,—*Can* we trust Jesus too fully for everything that his Word sets before us? Have we not often seen a trembling, anxious sinner put away from him the cup of a free salvation, lest it should be "presumption" to take it just as he was? Was not the presumption in daring to refuse what God had put to his very lips,—the waters of Life? Have not we bent all the prayerful energies of our souls, to teach him that what God *gave* him, it would be presumption to reject because of his own unfitness? Did we not specially press upon him that remission of sins is received by *faith*, and that to try to make himself worthy was to reject Christ now, and to dare to attempt partly to meet the claims of God's holiness himself?

You have done this, probably, scores of times, and now, my brother, suffer me, though but a "little one," to point your heart in the same way to Scripture warrant for receiving by faith, not only forgiveness of sins, but inward purity of soul. Christ gave Himself for you, that He might redeem you from ALL iniquity, and *purify* you unto Himself a peculiar person, zealous of good works. When is this redemption? *Now.* From what? ALL iniquity. What else does his sacrifice propose to you? To *purify* you unto Himself. When ought you to receive the redemption? Now. And when this purification? Equally NOW! How? By simple faith.

If my poor words present difficulties to your

heart, dear reader, I beg you to take some prayer from God's Word, upon which the Holy Spirit has flashed its light, as expressing the deep needs of your soul. Let the theories of your head go, and permit your heart to go out to God in faith, thus guided by the Word. If you are mourning over inward corruption, what can be more simple than to pray, "Create *in me* a clean heart, O God, and renew a right spirit within *me*." Can you doubt that such a petition, originating in God and returning to Him in the cries of one of His needy children, *honestly* offered in the name of Jesus, would be answered by the grace of a clean heart and a right spirit?

A CHRISTIAN PHYSICIAN.

A "beloved Physician," the story of whose work of faith and labor of love is scarcely second to that of George Muller in interest and power, writes,—

"O how my heart once yearned to *know* this 'victory that overcometh the world!' I remember a few years ago, in reading II. Thess. 2, I came to the 13th verse, where Paul says, 'We are bound to give thanks always to God for you, brethren, beloved of the Lord, because God hath from the beginning chosen you to salvation, through *sanctification* of the Spirit and belief of the truth.' *Through sanctification of the Spirit.* Here I paused, and read it over and over again, praying that God would sanctify me wholly by the Spirit. This verse comforted me many, many days. I felt that it was blessed to my soul, but the fullness of its meaning was not yet revealed to me. The inward currents of my heart were not stayed. I could not '*stand fast* therefore in the liberty wherewith Christ hath made us free,' for I was 'entangled again' and again 'with the yoke of bondage.' I could not 'reckon' myself 'dead' to the perplexities and irritations of daily life, which a heart yearning for purity condemns as dishonoring to God. More earnestly than ever, and many times a day, I prayed for strength to overcome, but found no rest to my soul, until I stopped praying for strength to overcome, and *gave myself wholly tc God to be kept.*

"At this time the Lord revealed to me in a wonderful manner, in all its majesty, the power of the prayer which He taught us to use, 'Our Father which art in Heaven: hallowed be Thy name.

Thy kingdom come. Thy will be done on earth, as it is in Heaven. Give us this day our daily bread; And forgive us our debts, as we forgive our debtors. And lead us not into temptation, but *deliver us from evil*: For Thine is the kingdom, and the power, and the glory, for ever. Amen.' O how my soul was filled, as I realized for the first time that it was His power that was to keep me!—for 'Thine *is* the power.'

"The work was all done then,—no more striving, no more praying for *strength* to overcome, but simply day by day, 'Jesus *keep* me, for Thine is the *power* and the glory,' and there *I rest* and am *kept*.

"I give this little record of personal experience, hoping that many who desire, but who have not gained 'the victory which overcometh the world, even our faith,' as they pray, 'Lead us not into temptation, but deliver us from evil, for Thine is the power,' may realize in all its fullness that the *power* belongs to Him who says He is 'able to keep you from falling.'"

The Psalmist says, "Thy Word have I hid *in mine heart*, that I might not sin against Thee."

Let any Christian, instead of handling the promises of God as abstractions, take them as the divine seed,—"spirit" and "life," as our Lord terms them; let him select some one beatitude, command, or promise, that embodies his soul's special need; let him believe that it contains God's covenant to himself; let him search out other sayings of God corresponding with this text; let him pray over it continually, morning, noon, and night, and even amid the busy scenes of his calling; let him continually raise his heart to God in supplication and trust; let him seek to exhaust the possibilities of faith and prayer, concentrating all the divinely-imparted energies of his soul on the particular truth embodied in the text; and let him not weary in well-doing, fully trusting that in due season he will reap if he faints not;—and he then shall find the power of Jehovah Himself pledged to the fruit-bearing of the seed thus sown and watered by faith and prayer.

"Forever, O Lord, Thy Word is settled in the Heaven!" and sooner shall this vast universe fail in its orbits and sink into remediless ruin, than a single promise of the eternal God fail toward one of his little ones, who has thus in faith committed the keeping of his soul to Him in well-doing as unto a faithful Creator.

God grant that this interview upon paper may be to His glory, and that He may open your heart to attend to these things spoken by Paul, as He did that of Lydia.

I trust that your prayers may go up with my own to God for a blessing on this intercourse, that whatever be God's truth, we may both know and live it to his glory. In this aspiration, and hoping that you will "suffer the word of exhortation," I am, your brother in Jesus.

CHAPTER III.

A WAY IN CHRIST.

TO all his other blessings our heavenly Father has added this, that his gifts, calling, and grace, are all "*in Christ Jesus*, who of God is made unto us wisdom, and righteousness, and sanctification, and redemption; that, according as it is written, 'He that glorieth, let him glory in the Lord.'"

Chalmers speaks finely of "the expulsive power of a new affection;" and that love is indeed expulsive in its character at first, all who have been deeply moved, in whatever way, well know. But they also know that when a new emotion has a little spent its energies, there comes a reaction, proportioned oftentimes to the greatness of the emotion. In this way is explained, and correctly, the condition of failure that follows the warmth and earnestness of the "first love" of Christians. Feeling a painful void at the time present, their hearts turn *to the memory of an emotion*, and that memory is cherished till it becomes a substitute for present, living faith. Or if this snare be severed, they depend on new discoveries in the truth of God, to maintain, by the light they inspire, the devotion of their souls. Alas! that men will put His gifts between themselves and the living, life-inspiring Christ.

The almost universal character of this experience shows plainly that there is something wanting in their knowledge of Christ, since the gospel itself is not a failure, to perfect the walk of believers.

I was asked to preach lately to a congregation where the deacon, in stating the needs of the members, remarked. "We have just enough religion among us to make us miserable." Nor did I wonder at his homely expression; for instead of casting themselves upon Christ to sanctify, as He had already justified them, they had been led to look for power for holiness of walk, too exclusively from the peace resulting from their knowledge of final salvation, from the responsive love that *ought* to spring up in their hearts, because of their known "judicial standing," and from the emotions which, were they unfallen beings, would continually fill their hearts with lively gratitude for infinite favors bestowed.

Well, indeed, might they feel "miserable," as they contrasted what they knew *ought* to be the love and devotedness of their hearts, with their actual wandering affections and palsied efforts to serve God. It is enough to make any one possessing any tenderness of conscience "miserable" to live in the unvarying sense of failure, his heart so often condemning him for sinning, and without the hope that he shall ever in this life really please God in his walk. Nor does the fact that there has been offered a divine atonement sufficient to meet all the future judgment of these failures, bring the relief that the soul needs, while it expects nothing else than to go on sinning all its days.

"Every breath I draw is sin," was the extreme statement made to me by a Christian professing full confidence in the sacrifice of Christ, and seeking to live in separation from the world. I fear he was right. Every breath *is* sin to him, if he has not faith to live without it; for "whatsoever is not of faith is sin." If sin be the inevitable, constant condition of the Christian, then is redemption "from all iniquity" transferred to the next life; abiding in Christ a hopeless attainment; to "sin not" a grievous command; and pleasing

God now, an impossibility. The very assurance of being begotten of God, and the prospect of an eternity in his presence, make the present condition of sinning "miserable," yea, agonizing, to a heart happily not entirely hardened by the continual sense of transgression. To believe in, and, in some degree, to love God, and yet to be among those who "cannot cease from sin," may well weigh the soul down with sorrow.

Some resource must be found to meet this. Like the wandering sheep, who, though set with his face homewards, will, as shepherds tell us, always choose a wrong path, if such can be found, rather than the one that leads to the fold; so, instead of going directly to Christ, as my wisdom to guide, my practical power of righteousness to live by, my sanctification of spirit, soul, and body, and my blessed, present redemption from all iniquity, I formerly turned from Christ, who is *both "the Way" and the entrance into it,* to adopt a system which puts off all those blessed offices of Christ in their full virtue, as intended for another state of existence; persuading myself that, "judicially," I was without spot and blameless, while in reality I was spotted all over like a leopard, and under often recurring condemnation for inward, even when not for outward, sins. The atonement of my Lord became to me too much of a theological doctrine, rather than the glorious effective reality which I now find it to be, meeting fully every *present* need of my soul.

Were anything revealed to man as "the power of God," we should expect it to overcome the world and all the powerful things in it, inasmuch as it would be the power of God in direct conflict with the powers of the world, the flesh, and the devil. None would deny the power thus revealed being capable of overcoming all else. The only question would be, whether God intended to do it in this stage of existence for those who trusted Him for it; and this being granted, there would remain but the question of the means and their use.

In the opening of Paul's first letter to the Corinthians, he states that the preaching of the cross of Christ is "the power of God unto us which are saved;" and that, while a crucified Christ is to the legalist a stumbling-block, and to the worldly wise foolishness, to those who are called, Christ is "the power of God and the wisdom of God." That through Christ's death on the cross, and his resurrection-life in the soul, God has provided a power capable of conforming the children of the kingdom to the image of its Head, few will venture to deny. The difficulty seems to come in when any *confess* that, having by faith availed themselves of these resources in Christ, they find their hearts "purified by faith," cleansed "from all unrighteousness," and, in keeping his word, "the love of God perfected" in their souls, (1 John ii. 5,) to the limit of present consciousness.

Thomas Walsh testified, "The Lord gives me to drink of his love as out of a river. I lay down, but could not sleep, through a deep and comfortable sense of the love of Christ. His Spirit rested on me, and made my heart flame with love to my God and my all. It never entered into my heart to conceive of thus loving Him with all the heart till He revealed it unto me by his Spirit. The fire of divine love burned incessantly in my soul." President Edwards said of Abigail Hutchinson, "She had from day to day such a sense of the glory of Christ and of God in his various attributes, that it seemed to me she dwelt for days together in a kind of beatific vision, and seemed to have as immediate intercourse with Him as a child with a father."

Has God provided any less privilege in Christ for you, my brother? Are *you* willing to put by everything else, including your preconceived opinions, to receive this fullness of the blessing of the gospel of Christ?

I confess to a tender, sincere sympathy with those who, beyond many around them, have been devoted to God, who have been used by God in his service in saving sinners or teaching saints, and who yet are unable to find anything in their own experience corresponding to what is confessed by some. Reading such narratives in the light of their own history, or by a system modified, it may be, to meet the requirements of this consciousness of continual sinning, these experiences seem to them egotistical and boastful. Instead of getting "out of self into Christ," they fear that their brethren are getting out of Christ into self again. This fear arises from not understanding that, in confessing themselves to be made "dead to sins and alive unto righteousness," their brethren are confessing simply that for which Christ bare their sins in His own body on the tree, as being accomplished in their souls. (See carefully 1 Pet. ii. 24, and 2. Cor. v. 17, 18.) Surely the words, "Christ liveth in me," and "For me to live is Christ," cannot mean *less* than the habitual victory over sin.

Suffer me, my brother, to recall your own experience in the remission of sins. Its distinctive feature was, that you trusted Christ for your present felt need of soul, and *what you trusted him for you received.* What your soul needed was remission of sins, and after having in vain sought it by efforts of your own, you found it in faith, apart from all effort, a simple receiving from God. The Holy Spirit quickened your soul to a sense of your need of pardon, and then satisfied the desires thus begotten in you, by showing you the sacrifice of Christ.

You must agree with us, that whatever the Holy Spirit makes us to yearn for, Christ came to give. Now substitute "purity of heart," "holiness," being "filled with the Spirit," whole-hearted "love to God and your neighbour," or "righteousness," for the pardon you once felt the need of; satisfy yourself that the Word sets either of these privileges before you as a gift for which the Holy Ghost is making you to hunger and thirst; then seek this blessing, not by efforts of your own, —not as a doctrine, not in imitating an experience of another, not in an emotion, but *in the Lord Jesus Christ through faith*,—and who then shall limit the extent to which your desires shall be satisfied? And when "filled with the fruits of righteousness, which are by Jesus Christ, unto the glory and praise of God," who shall then hinder you from proclaiming what the Lord hath done for your soul?

In no way so effectually as by following the example of Paul, in freely declaring what Christ has done for and in you, can you lead others to the same all-powerful Saviour. "The husbandman that laboureth must be first partaker of the fruits," and the Lord's witnesses must witness that they themselves experience what they teach. Satan's kingdom is not much disturbed by preaching which tells men that they ought to "go up and possess the land," while the preacher has to confess that he has not done so, thus giving "an evil report of the land," and practically saying, "We are not able to go up against the people; for they be stronger than we." God give us leaders like Caleb, who say, "Let us go up at once to possess it; for we are well able to overcome it;" men of the faith of Paul, who "can do all things through Christ strengthening" and who will at

God's command blow the ram's horn till the Canaanite walls fall down.

The British ambassador was a true man, though he told the incredulous Eastern despot, who had never been where water froze, that in his country they walked on hardened water, and though he was dismissed as a liar. Our testimony ought to be credited, at least by Christians, when we affirm that in the path where we tread, Christ is both able and willing to sustain us to the utmost limit of our faith, even though to the eye of sense, only unstable water be visible. None are so manifestly and pitiably weak as the "little children" of the kingdom, when without the presence of Christ; but none so strong as they who, *without reserve abandon themselves perfectly to Christ to live in them*, perfecting his strength in their weakness.

I know your love for the Lord and his cause, my brother. I know the virtue—the earnest, manly effort—that you have added to your faith. I know, by my own former experience, the unsatisfactoriness of the *current* of your inward life, even though you have seasons of joy, when the Lord comes to you as one that tarrieth for a night, and abideth not. I know that God has given you hungerings and thirstings after righteousness, so that you might even speak of "gnawings of hunger;" and that they were not given to tantalize you, but that you might so receive Christ as to have them satisfied.

Now, that you have not gone to him aright is evident, or you would have been "filled." I will, in true Christian love, use great plainness of speech. *You* have failed,—*not Christ.* I feel confident that the point of your failure is in not having committed unreservedly everything to Christ, in perfect self-abandonment. If I do not hold my ALL,—spirit, soul, and body,—committed to Him, I am walking with heavy weights, and miserable. Sometimes, becoming conscious of a weight, before unsuspected, I find it a sore effort to part with it; but my soul is in bondage till it is laid aside. Then it rises free before God. Try this, my brother, this laying aside *every* weight—THE VERY LAST ONE, whether it be care, or transgression, and you will then rise into the cloudless atmosphere where God's light can shine down upon you unhindered, where you no longer frustrate the grace of God, and where you can know "Christ formed in you."

Practical sanctification and purity of soul, with the consciousness of them, are as surely God's gift as is the forgiveness of sins; but the method is faith. It is a calling, and *in Christ.* It is a grace, and this grace "came by Jesus Christ."

Apart from Christ, we are instruments of unrighteousness to sin, as my hand is a rotting piece of flesh apart from my heart and brain. But, joined to Christ, we become instruments of righteousness unto God, just as my hand is full of life by its connexion with my heart, and rightly guided by its connexion with my brain. The thickness of a piece of paper will sever my hand's connexion with heart and brain, and yet the union may be maintained through a lifetime without interruption. It is just in this way that all our life, our strength, our righteousness, is *in Christ,* not in ourselves, except as we are receiving from Christ. We are not only weak, and poor, and helpless, but we are *nothing,* absolutely nothing apart from Christ. Yet *in Him* we have all things. O! blessed union, which joins us to the living heart and living Head, each one members in particular of the ONE body. O! miracle of grace, which gives us life for death, and incorruptibleness for corruption. Since faith is the channel of communicable life, O Lord, increase our faith!

> "If our faith were but more simple,
> We should take Him at His word;
> And our lives would be all sunshine
> In the sweetness of the Lord."

THE ACTRESS AND HOME MISSIONARY.

While addressing a company in one of the mission-houses in New York, I noticed a young woman much affected. I found after the meeting that she was an actress who had been brought to the point of turning her back on all her past life; but she was unable to believe that such a sinner as she was *could* receive the grace that was set before her. To my explanations of the divine sacrifice for sinners she only exclaimed,

"O yes, sir,—I know that it's all true, but I can't believe that it is *for me*."

It seemed too great "presumption" for her to believe that all her sins were blotted out, and she at once placed in the family of God. I left her in this condition of mind, longing for salvation, and yet too faithless to believe that it was for her.

It was very instructive to see immediately afterward a striking illustration that upon whatever level we may be walking, the same failure of faith to take the grace intended for us may be found. *Lack of faith to receive from God, is the sin that doth so easily beset us, and lies at the root of every failure, all the way from the first quickening of the Spirit, onward to the highest altitudes of devotedness and service to God.*

Upon parting with the actress, I was introduced to a refined, matronly, Christian woman, who, I understood, was giving her life to this gospel work among the abandoned. Her whole heart was in her work with an energy and simplicity that I have never seen surpassed. Her joy was to spend her years in the midst of this moral leprosy, raising the cross among the dying souls around her. But even while thus laboring for Christ, she was feeling most deeply her need of some privilege greatly beyond her present experience. So in earnest was she that she had just passed a sleepless night of sorrow and of prayer, for the full and satisfying revelation of Christ, with the *complete* victory over her own will. She knew that her sins had been forgiven her, and that she truly loved Jesus. Work for Jesus was the most delightful thing in the world to her.

"Sacrifices" were to her only privileges; but she mourned over the remaining evil of her own soul. She hungered for righteousness, and was not filled; the fountain of her heart, which ought only to well up with sweet waters, sent forth both bitter and sweet. She knew that there was in the gospel a redemption "from *all* iniquity;" but she had not found it. She knew that Christ bore her sins that she might become "dead to sin, and alive to righteousness," but she had not attained to it. If work, as some suppose, could bring a full blessing, surely it would have been found here. But her need was one which work could not supply.

The secret of this unsupplied need was soon found. Full of faith for God's work in others, and up to a certain point in herself, she needed to open the door of her heart yet more widely that the King of Glory might come in. This dear saint, who had so often taught the lesson, to anxious sinners, of faith, as the means of blessing, now saw that the very same lesson was to be learned by herself upon a different level. The very words that a few moments before had been said to the awakened actress,—*trust in Christ for what her soul felt the need of*,—were now to be applied to herself. She had prayed for inward holiness and full victory over sin, without faith to receive the immediate answer in Jesus.

Unbelief was the obstacle to the full answer, just as in the prayer for mercy from the awakened sinner. To sinner and saint alike, upon whatever level, unbelief is the bar, while faith is the channel of God's blessing. When Christians pray for full cleansing of soul and deadness to sin, the answer is unto them exactly according to their faith or their unbelief. Full faith gives the full deliverance; partial faith the partial victory. So much faith, so much deliverance, no more, no less! *If we would live up to the gospel standard of holiness, we must believe up to the gospel standard of faith*. Every complaint of leanness, failure, or sinning, is but a confession of want of belief. The stream can ascend no higher than the passage that conveys its waters from the fountain. Faith is the channel. While the fountain is infinite in depth and in height, its flow is regulated by the channel opened for it.

Shortly after this interview, the actress found in Christ, through faith, pardon for all her sins, and the missionary upon her high level of Christian experience also *found in Christ, through faith*, cleansing "from all unrighteousness." Faith in each grasped the promise, "My God shall supply all your need, according to his riches in glory *by Christ Jesus.*"

May what is here written in prayer be also read in prayer! "We pray always for you that our God would count you worthy of his calling, and fulfill *all* the good pleasures of his goodness, and *the work of faith with power*, that the name of our Lord Jesus Christ may be glorified in you, and ye in Him, according to the grace of our God, and the Lord Jesus Christ."

CHAPTER IV.

A WAY HID FROM MERE INTELLECT, AND REVEALED BY THE SPIRIT TO THE SOUL HUNGERING FOR RIGHTEOUSNESS.

THERE is a path which no fowl knoweth, and which the vulture's eye hath not seen: the lion's whelps have not trodden it, nor the fierce lion passed by it. . . . . The gold and the crystal cannot equal it. . . . . God understands the way thereof, and He knoweth the place thereof." Whatever may be the primary application of these words, they well express the closing of the way of holiness to every effort of the intellect. The consciousness of almost the whole race, sinners as well as "professors," is against it; for error is always with the many in these evil days; and however much men may differ about other things, they are nearly all agreed as to the impossibility of living without sin. "Eye hath not seen, nor ear heard, neither have entered into the heart of man, the things which God hath prepared for them that love Him. But God *hath* revealed them unto us by his Spirit; for the Spirit searcheth all things, yea, the deep things of God."

These things prepared by God are not all postponed to a future scene, but are even now spiritually discerned. We are neither surprised nor disappointed, much as we may be pained, when the testimony to the present fullness of blessing is rejected. To some the Sun of righteousness has already arisen with healing in his wings, in a sense never before known, albeit the mists of educational prejudice or doctrinal system may hide his rays from the vision of those around them. We therefore intreat you dispassionately, prayerfully, and humbly, to seek wisdom of God, whether these things be so.

"The blood" is the meritorious and only ground upon which any of God's blessings can reach us without frustrating the eternal justice of the Ruler of the universe, but the means selected by God are the indwelling and guidance of the Holy Spirit. First the blood, then the anointing oil,—forgiveness, and then cleansing. Were the merit and power of the blood more fully applied by faith, then would the power of the Holy Ghost in Christians be more known.

The perpetual prayer of the Church of England is, "Almighty God unto whom all hearts are open, all desires known, and from whom no secrets are hid; cleanse the thoughts of our hearts by the inspiration of the Holy Spirit, *that we may perfectly love Thee,* and worthily magnify Thy holy name." Connect this with the soul-inspiring words of our blessed Lord in Mark xi. 22–24: "Have the faith of God. For verily I say unto you, That whosoever shall say unto this mountain, Be thou removed, and be thou cast into the sea; and shall not doubt in his heart, but shall believe that those things which he saith shall come to pass; he shall have whatsoever he saith. Therefore I say unto you, What things soever ye desire, when ye pray, believe that ye receive them, and ye shall have them." And again: "All things whatsoever ye ask in prayer, believing, ye shall receive." After half a century of experience of the power of this promise, the apostle is enabled to add by the Holy Ghost: "And this is the confidence that we have in Him, that if we ask anything according to his will, He heareth us. And if we know that He hear us, whatsoever we ask, we know that we have the petitions we desired of Him." "And whatsoever we ask, we receive of Him because we keep his commandments, and do those things that are pleasing in his sight."

The only question would then seem to be, whether "the first and great commandment," as recited by the Lord Jesus—"Thou shalt love the Lord thy God with all thy heart, and with all thy soul, and with all thy mind"—is included in the "righteousness of the law," which is to be "fulfilled in us, who walk not after the flesh, but after the Spirit." How strange that we should ever have doubted it! We ask, then, according to God's will when we *believingly* pray, "Cleanse Thou our hearts by the inspiration of thy Holy Spirit, that we may perfectly love Thee, and worthily magnify thy holy name!" And when the petition is granted, who shall say that it is presumption to affirm that our prayers have been answered? The acknowledgment is "glorying in the Lord" as truly as the owning that we are saved from future wrath.

Is it not strange that God's children can mock their Father in heaven by asking for things that they do not expect to receive—shall we say hardly really desire—in this life? and that, themselves too faithless to be able to receive full answers to their prayers, they should be grieved by those who say that they have asked, and have received what they prayed for. I confess to have been myself once stumbled by a dear brother saying that he did indeed love God with all his heart, soul, and mind. Of his exterior holiness of life none could doubt, for we have never known any one who seemed so uniformly filled with the Spirit. It was the testimony of an inmate of his family that his *whole* life was consumed in praise, prayer, and working for God. Measuring his faith and blessing by my own little measure, I thought that there must be some self-delusion; but when it pleased God, in answer to months of prayer, to open in power to my soul that word, "He that dwelleth in love dwelleth in God, and God in him," I found to my own surprise and joy that it was the Spirit's work so to fill my poor wavering soul, that, *so far as I was conscious*, I did and do now love God with my whole heart, soul, and mind. I ask to be preserved from ever again judging of the faith of others by my own smaller measure. It is "*according to the riches of his glory*," and not according to man's limits, that God fills his trusting children "with might by his Spirit in the inner man."

Many a tender soul that loves the Lord finds its acutest suffering in the consciousness of a divided heart and wandering affection, so that it has often in substance exclaimed—

> "'Tis worse than death my God to love,
> And not my God alone!"

As in many congregations true lovers of God are kept bound hand and foot in grave-clothes by the teaching all around them, that it is presumption in any one that is not dying to be sure of going to heaven: so now are many precious and tender souls restrained by the grave-clothes of the doctrine that habitual sinning is the inevitable condition of God's own saved saints, and that the command to love the Lord with our whole heart, soul, and mind, can only be fulfilled through death,—that the bride may not *wholly* love her husband till her heart is about to be stilled in the grave. May the same divine voice which, in our death in trespasses and sins, said to us "Come forth!" be also effectually heard saying, "*Loose him and let him go!*" Let the taste and atmosphere of a past death pass away with the bestowal of "life more abundantly." He who spake by a human voice to Lazarus is speaking through Christendom to his saints by his Spirit, and giving us by his divine power "all things that pertain to life and godliness, through the knowledge of Him who hath called us to glory and virtue," and making us "partakers of the divine nature, *having escaped the corruption that is in the world through lust.*"

There is one point in this subject which we find from letters received, is not understood, though repeatedly stated. When the Christian thus puts on the Lord Jesus Christ, or recognizes Him living in his heart, and reigning in victory over sin, he is not thereby made complete in understanding, or in judgment, or in doctrine. He simply is placed where he by faith receives from God power to act day by day up to the given measure of light upon his duty. It is the power of overcoming all *discerned* evil that is bestowed; and as the Spirit enlightens the conscience (or *consciousness*) from time to time faith gives the victory. "Beloved, *if our hearts condemn us not,* then have we confidence toward God." This is all that is claimed.

To-morrow I may discern evil in things in

which to-day I am living without condemnation. Were the sight of angels given us, we could scarcely take one step in our mingled surroundings. It has not pleased God to reveal at once either the whole measure of his grace and power, or the whole nature of the evil things around us. This principle is clearly stated by Paul. "Let us therefore, *as many as be perfect*, be thus minded, and if in anything ye be otherwise minded, God shall reveal even this unto you. Nevertheless, whereto we have already attained, let us walk by the same rule; let us mind the same thing." A heathen converted last week may be now walking up to the standard to which he has "already attained," and yet be in practices from which a further knowledge of God's will shall separate him. Through all the steps of his advance he may, through Christ, have no stain on his conscience (or knowledge). Thank God! there *is* provided in Christ, who lives in the heart by faith, power to walk from day to day without blame before God in love, in fulfilment of every duty as progressively revealed.

The divine principle to a Christian is,—"Whatsoever is not of faith is sin," and conversely whatsoever is of faith is not sin. "Without faith it is impossible to please God," but with faith it is possible to please God. I breathe to-day the atmosphere of the love of God, every past sin forgiven, and through the blood of cleansing, without a present sense of transgression,—not a cloud to separate me from God; but I may not be able to walk to-morrow with a clear conscience in all the paths I tread to-day. Nevertheless I am to-day walking in the light, having fellowship with God, and knowing that the blood of Jesus Christ, His Son, cleanseth me from all sin. This might be termed a Christian, not a Divine, nor an angelic nor yet an Adamic "perfection;" but those who by faith enter into its privileges may overcome the world, and be conscious that up to the present capacity of the poor, weak vessel, they are filled with the Spirit.

The great practical question is—not the metaphysics of sin,—but *what pleases God;* and what pleases Him should satisfy the believer's heart. Enoch, in a dispensation that was scarcely as the dawn to our own glorious day, "pleased God," and surely our privileges in resurrection-life are not below those of Enoch. John was able to say,

"We keep his commandments, and do those things that are pleasing in his sight," and God is working in some hearts and lives "that which is well-pleasing in his sight, through Jesus Christ."

It follows from this that persons who have great light in the teaching of Scripture may be walking outwardly in advance of the sanctified but ignorant Christian, while yet the one is sinning and under a sense of condemnation, and the other, more ignorant but more trusting, walks with a conscience void of offence. The understanding of "all mysteries and all knowledge" would be but a poor equivalent for the simple faith that always takes Jesus for all that He reveals Himself, and so finds present victory.

To "be filled with the Spirit" is one of Christ's "commanding promises and promising commands." It is connected with the warning to the Ephesians not to allow themselves to be carried beyond their natural condition by the stimulus of wine, but rather to be filled with the Spirit, that psalms, hymns, and spiritual songs should fill their mouths, while they made melody in their hearts to the Lord. The apostles, when filled with the Spirit, had to defend themselves from the charge of drunkenness, and those who yield themselves up to be filled by the Spirit may, to an unbelieving world, or to cold-hearted, sinning professors, seem like men "filled with new wine," or appear to them as David did to Michal, when he danced before the ark, even though God hath given them the "Spirit of power, and of love, and of a sound mind."

The great hindrance to being "filled with the Spirit" is the pre-occupation of the heart with worldliness or sin, so that room is not left for the manifestation of the Spirit. God's Spirit is the Spirit of Holiness, and it cannot dwell with sin, or even with the love of the world. I tremble for "professors of religion" as I read these words, "If any man love the world, the love of the Father is not in him." "He that hath my commandments, *and keepeth them,* he it is that loveth Me;" and "If any man love not the Lord Jesus Christ, let him be Anathema Maran-atha." I thank God that I have not to determine to whom they apply.

We are solemnly warned that "*they that are in the flesh* cannot please God;" and the Word adds, "But ye are not in the flesh, but in the Spirit, if so be that the Spirit of God dwell in you. Now if any man have not the Spirit of Christ, he is none of his." And it adds the text, "*And if Christ be in you the body is dead because of sin;* but the Spirit is life because of righteousness." "For if ye live after the flesh, ye shall die; but if ye, through the Spirit, do mortify the deeds of the body, ye shall live." The words are God's, not ours. Shall we turn the edge of these solemn tests to professing Christians by vainly trying to conform them to some theological system? Or shall we receive them in their solemn and deeply searching lessons, rousing us from every sleep of false security?

When God by the Spirit leads any one into this humble and clean condition, where the whole power of the atonement is by faith received, then, emptied of all else, he can be filled with the Spirit. What is needed is this emptying of all self-merit, self-effort, self-worship, self-guidance, self-praying, and self-acting. As the air rushes into a vacuum, so the Spirit must fill the soul emptied of self. The great need of our time is Holy Ghost power in our ministry. There is many a professor as harmless to Satan's kingdom as the cannon-ball that the child rolls across the floor. But put the power behind it, and it will fly like lightning on its mission of destruction to the strongholds of the devil. There is many a rusting locomotive, a mere obstruction in the way. Apply but the steam to it, and it would draw thousands heavenward.

Without the almighty power of the Holy Ghost, preaching is but the sounding brass and tinkling cymbal. Oh! my brother, what would you not give to have this power of God that will make you a flaming herald of the gospel, imparting to your soul at all times the unction and power of the Holy Ghost, so that God's purposes should be always accomplished in and by you? God does not so much ask you to give, as to *receive*. Do not "frustrate the grace of God," which now in this stream of full and present salvation is flowing around you. Erect no barriers to its waters,—hinder no drop of its fulness from covering your soul. Take Jesus *now* for all that He presents Himself to you as able to do, yielding yourself without the smallest reservation a living sacrifice, made holy by the altar on which your thank-offering is laid. When you have done this, do not shrink from owning yourself among the holy brethren, who lift up holy hands without wrath *or doubting* to the holy God, from whom you have that command—possible to faith only, but to faith surely possible—"BE YE HOLY, FOR I AM HOLY."

A MANUFACTURER,

a Christian who had for many years been preaching Christ a Saviour for sinners, while yet he found himself living under a painful sense of inward corruption, remarked, among the workmen under his care, a few who seemed different from the professors around them, in that they seemed so filled with the Spirit, so much in prayer, and bearing into the workshops such a uniform sweet savour of Christ. These men, closely associated with their employer in Gospel work, often pressed upon him the privilege of a present, practical, full sanctification in Christ. Against this doctrine he had the strongest prejudice, constantly opposing it by every argument as a dangerous heresy.

At the solicitation of one of these Christians he set apart an evening to examine with him the Scriptures upon the subject, and being versed in theological argument he was able to silence the explanations of the praying workman. Sometimes a different reading or translation seemed to break the power of the text urged upon him ; sometimes another meaning could be got out of it ; and, sometimes, where there was no other escape, it was interpreted in a forensic or judicial sense, with a denial of its practical application. The pious workman, conscious, notwithstanding all the arguments, that Christ was formed in his own soul, closed the interview sadly, feeling that though overcome by argument, no one could take from him the living, blessed reality of faith that did overcome the world, the flesh, and the devil.

Not long after, he one day said to his employer . "When in the morning I *entirely trust* my soul to the keeping of Jesus, relying on Him *alone* to be preserved from transgression through the day, He always answers my faith and *does* keep me from known sin."

This simple testimony from an honest God-fearing Christian, went home to the heart of the reasoner. Where argument failed, a faithful witnessing prevailed. He had denied it as a *doctrine*, but he could not gainsay so simple and scriptural an *experience* of faith. "*Can it be true?*" he said to himself. The clouds of a deficient theological system were pierced, and like a gleam of sunshine over his soul, came the blessed hope that his life might become a victory where it had been a failure, holy where it had been unholy, blameless where it had been sinful.

Prayer and the study of the Scriptures now seemed to open the very heavens to his soul. Instead of asking Christ to *help* him, he now handed everything over to his Saviour, to *do* for and in him. When temptation assailed him, as one would put a screen between his face and a scorching fire, just so by faith he uniformly placed Christ between him and the snare, and rejoiced in beholding his Saviour only, the temptation being shut out. His soul was filled with wonder as from day to day he thus found himself so fully delivered from his besetting sins.

The obstacle of unbelief, with its resulting transgressions, being thus taken away, there followed, some time after, while waiting upon his knees in silence before God, the wonderful baptism of the Spirit, in a power which he had never conceived possible in this life, and he became, and now remains, after several years, solemnly conscious of the fulfilment of that promise: "If a man love me, he will keep my words: and my Father will love him, and we will come unto him and make Our *abode* with him."

Thus, Christ, God's Way of holiness, hidden from his intellect, was revealed to his heart, even before he could clearly state the Scriptural doctrine as to "Holiness through Faith." Since then years have passed, bringing with them constantly enlarging blessings, both in the conversion of sinners and in the leading of saints into soul union with Christ,—tenfold beyond any ever known before. The Scriptures are now, from cover to cover, radiant with the doctrine of a present practical sanctification, as well as justification, *in Christ*. Both were received by the same simple faith.

"How Thou canst share Thy life with us,
Yet be the God Thou art,
Is darkness to my intellect,
But sunshine to my heart."

CHAPTER V.

IT EXALTS THE ATONEMENT OF OUR LORD.

IN this chapter, before writing which, I have waited for some weeks in special prayer for enlightenment and guidance on so solemn a subject, I desire to point out how greatly the atonement is exalted by trusting to it for a present salvation from sinning.

In the Epistle to the Hebrews, which deals so specially with the sacrificial aspect of our Lord's work, we find the various forms of the word "sanctify" more often than in all the other epistles combined. It was that Jesus "might *sanctify* the people with his own blood," that He "suffered without the gate." "For if the blood of bulls and of goats," the epistle argues, "and the ashes of an heifer sprinkling the unclean, sanctifieth to the purifying of the flesh; *how much more* shall the blood of Christ, who through the eternal Spirit offered Himself without spot to God, purge your conscience from dead works to serve the living God?" "Now once in the end of the world hath

He appeared to put away *sin* by the sacrifice of Himself."

Opening with the declaration of how Jesus takes his place as the fulfilment of every type, this epistle shows that the law made nothing perfect, but that there is *the bringing in of a better hope.* It further shows the continual sacrifices failing to "make the comers thereunto perfect," and then declares that we are, by the fulfilment of His will, "sanctified through the offering of the body of Jesus once for all." In harmony with all this we find the epistle concluding: "Now the God of peace, that brought again from the dead our Lord Jesus, that great Shepherd of the sheep, *through the blood of the everlasting covenant,* make you perfect in every good work to do his will, working in you that which is well pleasing in his sight, through Jesus Christ; to whom be glory for ever and ever."

It is because this sanctification, to which we bear testimony, is through the blood of Jesus, that we feel confidence in casting ourselves unreservedly upon Christ, to receive its accomplishment. The gospel has been too much preached as though Jesus had said, "Be thou convalescent: try not to sin," rather than, "Behold, thou art made whole: *sin no more.*" When the leper, kneeling, cried, "If thou wilt, thou canst make me clean," the compassionate reply followed at once, "I will; *be thou clean.*" It is the blood of Jesus Christ, applied to those who walk in the light, that now "cleanseth us from all sin;" and even should our feet for a moment stumble, it does not follow that we were not treading the highway of holiness; nor should we for a moment lose our confidence, but see to it that the same flash of consciousness which shows us our fall should also bring its confession, and, with the confession, the re-cleansing of the soul "from all unrighteousness." Nor will then the believing heart, even after so sad an event as a transgression, doubt its sanctification or fear its confession; for it hears the command, "What God hath cleansed, that call not thou common."

The subtlety of Satan is perhaps nowhere more shown than in stopping the saints short at one half the truth conveyed in passages of Scripture. Half-texts rob God's children of half their present joys and half their power of service, as well as half their future crowns for service. I preached for ten years on the words, ' Who his own self bare our sins in his own body on the tree," before I realized the expressed purpose of that sin-bearing to be, that we should become *actually*, and not as a mere figure of speech, "dead to sins and alive to righteousness." "Who gave Himself for us" was always a precious word; but the other half of the text was not received into my heart,—" to redeem us from all iniquity;" for such a *present* redemption was too much for my faith. However much I might rejoice in the atonement as washing away the stains made by sin, I had not learned to forego self confidence so entirely as to receive the blood as cleansing the fountain, the very source of evil thoughts, murders, and so on. I did not see that the reason that this fountain of the heart sent forth both sweet and bitter waters was, that the blood had not been allowed to manifest its full virtue in cleansing from all unrighteousness.

"The blood of Jesus Christ, his Son, cleanseth us from all sin" was probably more constantly on my lips than any single passage of Scripture for ten years, before I saw that its application was not primarily to cancelling the record of sin, but to the inward cleansing of the souls of those who "walk in the light as He is in the light." When a sinner is converted to God, he is brought to *Jesus the Light*, which shines upon and into him. If he then walks in the Light,—or in Jesus,—He shines through and through him, revealing hourly the things that are contrary to God and to holiness; and as they are revealed by the light, they are cleansed by the blood. *A walk in the true Light always leads to the blood of cleansing.* Thus we find that if we walk in the light as He is in the light, God and ourselves have fellowship one with another, and then we realize that the blood of Jesus Christ cleanseth us inwardly from all sin.

"Whatsoever doth make manifest is light, and all things that are reproved are made manifest by the light." Happy child of God, who, as from day to day he walks in the light, shall bring *everything* that is made manifest in his outward or inward life, to the fountain opened for sin and for uncleanness, and find himself thus hourly cleansed inwardly from all sin, and possessing a heart that, condemning him not, leaves him in confidence toward God.

Nothing short of this is walking in the light. It is solemn to remember that if any one *saith* that he has fellowship with God, and walks in darkness, he lies, and does not the truth. It is God that says so! Alas, how many around us are claiming to have fellowship with God, while yet they walk in darkness, with defiled consciences and stumbling steps! Would that I could say something to arouse them to the fact that *God must have realities.* "Awake to righteousness, *and sin not.*" Self-persuasion that we have fellowship in a simple recognition of the truth, is not a reality. The soul must yield itself up to the Holy Spirit, to be led in a walk in the light, where everything is given up to God, and everything received from God—where "all things are of God, who hath reconciled us to Himself by Jesus Christ. . . . For He hath made Him to be sin for us, who knew no sin, that we might be made the righteousness of God in Him."

In reply then to the question often asked us by dear brethren, who value the precious blood of Christ, and who feel a jealous fear lest it should be set aside or slighted, "If you are walking thus in the way of holiness, where is the need of blood?" we reply that we exalt the atonement far more than ever before. It is most blessed to bring the outward actions to the atonement for remission of sins, but is it not far more blessed to bring the inward being or soul to the cross, so that the body or root within us of all sinning may be kept continually in the place of death, and that putting on the new man, which after God is *created in righteousness and true holiness*, it alone may be alive and active?

Ah! beloved friends, there never was so much need of the blood as now, because it is only by that blood every moment applied that we can walk here. That blood was shed not only to wash away the stain which sins had left upon us, but to wash inwardly the sin itself away; and if I am not sinning at this moment, it is because the deep inbred sin of my nature, which would make it utterly impossible for me to please God, is being at this moment purged by the blood of Christ. And this seems to be the teaching in 1 John i. 7–10; ii. 1. We are told here that if we walk in the light, the blood of Jesus cleanseth from all sin, not only from the stains of sin, or the punishment of sin, but from sin itself. (1 John i. 7.)

This, however, must not make us think sin is eradicated otherwise than in our participation of

Christ. The angels themselves would instantly find corruption in their souls, were they separated from the great Source of life. We have no independent holiness. We are to be vividly alive to the fact, that it is only as we are every moment cleansed that we can at all walk in the light of God, who is of purer eyes than to behold iniquity (ver. 8). But this need not discourage us ; for if we confess our sins, He is faithful and just to forgive us our sins, and to cleanse us from all unrighteousness, and He does do it (ver. 9). As though a child by disobedience had fallen into the mire : the first thing is the confession, then the forgiveness, and then the stains are all washed out. And last of all, lest any from being thus cleansed should forget they had been sinners, we are again reminded of the sorrowful fact (ver. 10), but are at once told that these very things have been written to us "that we sin not." (ii. 1.)

Let us suppose that here is a spring of water which is poisoned in its very source, and which can of course therefore send forth none but poisoned waters. But a remedy is found which counteracts the poison, and makes the waters pure and sweet. That remedy is applied in the very source of the spring itself, and the waters *flow out* therefore pure and sweet. But they do so only so long as it is applied. The moment the remedy is stayed, that very moment the poisonous waters flow out as foul as ever. Now, this is what the blood of Christ does for us,—it reaches the very spring itself, "purifying *our hearts* by faith," cleansing us "from all filthiness of the flesh and spirit," and enabling us by faith to realize that wondrous statement that "every man that hath this hope in Him purifieth himself, even as He is pure." We purify ourselves, not by effort, but by faith ; not by works, but by the precious blood of Christ. This clean and humble condition, however, is ours only while the blood is applied by faith, for the very moment faith ceases to apply it, corruption ensues, and the same old bitter waters flow out.

It is mistaking the very meaning of the word to suppose that the blood of Christ cleanses only from the stains and guilt of sin, and that unless sins are committed we do not need its present application. We need it far more to *prevent* our sinning, than even to wash it away when committed. We need it to purge our consciences, to purify our hearts, to deliver us *from* our sins ; and we have a very faint conception of its infinite worth when we confine its power to cleanse, only to obliterating the record of our sins, and to washing away their stains.

The little stone by the road side receives dust from every passing wind. The shower has often cleansed it, but it has always become again soiled. Another stone of the same lustre lies near by, but within the brook. It is perpetually cleansed and kept clean by the flowing waters. Clouds of dust may pass over it, but they do not reach it, and it always reflects the clear rays of the sun. All its cleansing, all its purity is in the stream, not in itself.

There is no need, therefore, for continuing in sin in order that grace may abound ; for grace much more abounds in our being cleansed from sin, and hence obtaining a continual deliverance from it, since it is grace, and grace only, that does it all. And none know the worth of Jesus like those whose hearts have been opened to receive *all* the salvation He died to procure, even a salvation from sinning as well as a salvation from hell ;

nor can any sing with such a depth of meaning as these the simple yet precious words—

> "I'm a poor sinner, and nothing at all;
> But Jesus Christ is my All in all."

Oh, my brother, how shall you and I ever praise God enough for such a wonderful salvation, so manifested in the souls of those who will receive it by faith, and triumph through Christ, amid all the works of Satan, and in the presence of his apparently full victories in the world around us. Let us, therefore beware lest the atonement of our Lord be dishonored by too much limiting its results to the future world, thus making our Lord to accomplish in death what He is not willing to do in our life. Let us remember that whosoever confesses Christ with the mouth unto salvation, should also believe in his heart *unto righteousness*—practical righteousness—and that when we call Him by his name, the Lord Jesus Christ, we are supposed to believe of him that for which He is so called—King, Saviour, the Anointed. He is thus named because God sent Him to rule in his kingdom in our hearts,—to save us from (not in) our sins, and to purify unto Himself a holy priesthood.

I prayed long over that text, "They overcame him by the blood of the Lamb;" but, thank God, I know its meaning now by a blessed experience, that the blood of Christ cleanseth, not only the stream, but the fountain. I keep carefully to the word, "*cleanseth*," not *hath cleansed once for all*, but now cleanseth by the continual application of faith. From the cleansed heart, prepared for the manifestation of the Holy Ghost, must necessarily flow the fruits of the Spirit; for the blood of atonement and the oil of the Holy Spirit go together.

Were the life commencing in this walk of Christian holiness prolonged on earth a thousand years, and were it to progress indefinitely, each day learning and practising more perfectly the lessons of Christ, there would be realized at the close of such a life, yet more deeply than at its commencement, the need of the blood of Christ. We may build upon it, but never can we leave it behind, nor cease to need its merits as our only ground of confidence before God.

There is some fearful mistake when the same fountain is found to "send forth at the same place sweet water and bitter!"—when there come from the same heart love and hatred, joy and variance, peace and envying, longsuffering and wrath, gentleness and strife, faith and heresies, meekness and emulations; "out of the same mouth blessing and cursing." It is said of those "that are Christ's" that they *have* crucified the flesh, with its affections and lusts, not that these things continue alive.

The Lord grant you and me, if we "live in the Spirit," to "also walk in the Spirit," so continuously and entirely cleansed by the blood of Jesus, as that out of a perfect heart shall flow *only* rivers of living water, to the salvation and refreshment of many.

The Lord make you not faithless, but believing for larger blessing,—the "exceeding abundantly" —above all that you have ever asked or thought.

A PRESBYTERIAN MINISTER.

"I had been preaching with much joy one evening, during an awakening in a neighbouring church, on the text, 'The blood of Jesus Christ, His Son, cleanseth us from all sin,' and seeking to teach through it, to the sinners present, their privilege of immediate and full remission of sins, through the blood of Christ. On returning to my lodgings with a Christian brother, he spoke to me of his enjoyment of the address, and then went on to make some remarks on teaching half truths from half texts. He related how that for ten years he had constantly preached from the words, 'Who his own self bare our sins in his own body on the tree,' without ever teaching the complement in the last half of the verse: 'that we being *dead unto sins*, should live unto righteousness.' He had taught abiding in Christ, without its result of sinning not. He had often said 'Who gave himself for us,' without adding, 'that He might redeem us from *all* iniquity.' I was led to see that the text I had preached from was addressed to my own soul primarily, rather than to the sinners before me, and that it was myself who needed the lesson. The Holy Spirit opened to my understanding that if I, a Christian, would walk in the light, as God is in the light, I should have fellowship with Him in a sense little as yet conceived of, even amid all my earnestness; that I should know inwardly, as a blessed reality, that 'the blood of Jesus Christ cleanseth us from all sin;' and that all my groanings for deliverance from my inward corruptions, should be met by the fountain opened for sin and uncleanness. I cannot define fully the effect upon my own soul of the words of my friend, but never had I been filled with such precious views of the purifying power of Christ.

"This blessed view of the cleansing blood opened up more and more on my soul for two years —a period of prayerful investigation, and yet of anxiety lest my friend were not in error in his understanding of these texts. All this time I was praying God to show me my full privileges in Christ, but to save me from heresy. I met my friend several times in the railway cars, when he always earnestly set before me the fulness of present privilege that was in Christ, and at our command through faith, illustrating his views by Christian experience.

"At a conference meeting of Presbytery, it was one evening proposed to consecrate ourselves more definitely and fully to God, and the act was accompanied by a wonderful baptism of the Spirit, which opened to my soul the hope of the near consummation of my soul-longings. Shortly after this, I invited the brother who had opened these things to me, to address the church under my care.

At the close of his address, on being 'dead to sin, and risen with Christ,' I spoke to the people of the power of Christ to save from their sins all those who would fully consecrate themselves, and trust Him.

"During that week I was led to see, as never before, the privilege of an *entire* soul-rest in Christ, and that it was to be entered into by faith. On the Lord's day, I preached twice on this subject, from a full soul, and after the evening service I proposed to a Christian manufacturer that a few Christians should meet together the next day to enter into rest. I did not say to seek rest, but, so confident was my faith, '*to enter in.*' Ten earnest, godly men, mostly from his workshops, on the following day, knelt down in my friend's warehouse, among the boxes. We remained on our knees an hour and a quarter, in prayer, praise, and consecration. Of us, too, it might be said, 'And when they had prayed, the place was shaken where they were assembled together, and they were all filled with the Holy Ghost.'

"I have been conscious ever since that it was then and there that in a definite transaction with God, I entered into a complete soul-rest in Christ, a rest, through the cleansing blood, which my soul has never lost for one hour since. It was attended by the satisfying certainty that whatever spiritual blessings I thenceforth claimed in simple faith should be mine.

"Since then I have received answers to my prayers for holiness as never before. I have again and again realized more growth in one day, than before in a whole year. From that time my soul has been filled with a wonderful divine consciousness of the actual, in-wrought reality of the expression, 'I am crucified with Christ, nevertheless I live ; yet, not I, but Christ liveth in me.' Instead of pining for rest, I am continually praising God for realized rest, the deep, inward Sabbath-keeping of my blood-cleansed soul. I can now see no limit to the possibilities of the life of Christ in my soul, since I have accepted the atonement in its full purposes, both of pardon and holiness."

CHAPTER VI.

IT MUST MAKE THE SOUL VICTORIOUS OVER INWARD AS WELL AS OUTWARD SIN.

THERE is an experience, not universal, it may be, to all who profess the name of Jesus, but uniform, so far as my observation extends, in those who walk in the full, searching light of God, and who honestly bring their deeds to this light. The work of conversion has been unmistakable; the assurance of final salvation is unvarying; the apparent devotedness to God is exemplary; the joy in the study of the Word great; and the access to God in prayer at times soul-inspiring. This condition of soul may continue for years, and through watchfulness and prayer, outward sin may be mostly avoided. The heart finds, even though often overcome by inward evil, great happiness in working for Jesus. Though sometimes brought into sorrow for transgresssion, through sudden temptation, the sense of forgiveness is clear. And yet, through all these privileges, there is the continued and undefined, yet painful feeling, as though a cloud intervened between God and the soul,—a cloud which neither earnest, self-denying service, nor attainments, however large, in scriptural truth, are able wholly to dispel. Work is sometimes entered on, and even recommended, as a relief to this unrest. This uneasy sense of the lack of full, unhindered fellowship with God is the great sorrow of many, if not most Christian hearts.

But the plummet has not yet sounded to the depths of the soul: and to those who do not shrink from it, another step of faith is yet to be taken. Far down, deep below the current of the previous consciousness, while occupied with the intense activities of Christian life, there are the continual motions of *inward* sin. The spiritual vision now discovers a great sink of iniquity within, so that instead of "a pure heart," there is conscious inward impurity. The quickened and tender conscience is convicted by the Holy Spirit of a deep, in-wrought pollution, antecedent to any acts of sin. This, which had been a *doctrine* before, becomes now a soul-harrowing, conscious reality. Self-distrusting and self-renouncing before, the soul now becomes self-abhorring, and cries out "Create in me a *clean heart*, O God, and renew a *right spirit* within me!" It is not now so much a question of manifested sins, as of *sin* as their root, that the soul must grapple with. "Must I ever find within me an active fountain welling up bitter waters along with the sweet fruits of the Spirit? Am I to be for ever conscious of inward impurity? Is death alone to be my inward deliverer? Can I never call upon God out of a pure heart,—a heart *consciously* cleansed?" the soul now bitterly exclaims.

The Holy Spirit never creates hungerings and thirstings after righteousness but in order that Christ may fill the longing soul. These convictions of *inward* sin in a believer, so remarkable in their parallel to the work of conviction as to *outward* sins in an unbeliever, bring the saint a second time to the cross. Once it was forgiveness of sins for which the soul cried out; now it is cleansing—holiness. A holy intensity of desire to be indeed entirely the Lord's, and to find Christ formed within and reigning in resurrection-life over inward as well as outward sin, takes possession of the heart. Nothing can now satisfy it without the consciousness of having received that blessed result of the sin-bearing of Jesus, the "being *dead* to sins," and the *living* "unto righteousness" (see 2 Peter ii. 24)—inward and outward purity. The soul which before pleaded for the impossibility of ceasing from sin, and consoled its own consciousness of failure by the narratives of the failures of the saints, now rather uses them as warnings, and instinctively turns with indescribable longings to the highest standards of practical holiness that the Scriptures or the examples of saints present, and pleads THE BLOOD as the means of cleansing.

Glimpses of the possibilities of a different and a higher life burst through the clouds of sorrow for indwelling sin, that envelope the soul. All remnants of confidence in self-effort wither in the remembrance of past failure, and the awful sense of the holiness of God. The occasional soul-inspiring views of the scriptural standard of inward purity combine with the convictions of the Spirit of God, to bring the soul into an agony of self-despair, which finds vent in such language as "*Who* shall deliver me from the body of death?"

This is the very place to which the Holy Spirit has led the soul, and He who to all its former prayers for holiness seemed to have "answered not a word," now finds that it has reached the point of self-despair where these prayers for purity can be answered. It is then that the heart, unable to define its experience in the suddenness and the joy of its discovery of the present power of Jesus to save from sin, breaks out, "I thank God through Jesus Christ our Lord!" And thus, in the joyful sense that there is "now no condemnation to them that are in Christ Jesus," the soul goes on to realize that "the law of the Spirit of life in Christ Jesus hath made me free from the law of sin and death. For what the law could not do, in that it was weak through the flesh, God sending his own Son in the likeness of sinful flesh, and for sin, condemned sin in the flesh: THAT THE RIGHTEOUSNES OF THE LAW MIGHT BE FULFILLED IN US, WHO WALK NOT AFTER THE FLESH, BUT AFTER THE SPIRIT!"

Doth not the present heaven of privilege, in putting off the old man, and putting on the new man, *which after God is created in righteousness and true holiness*, burst through these inspired words, my brother, upon your soul?

He who has *thus* taken Christ finds a sweetness in communion never before experienced, and a victory over inward and outward sins that he never conceived of as possible for him in this life. The atonement becomes more intensely real than ever before, as the expression of the love of the Father. The solemn scene upon Calvary, God manifest in the flesh suffering for man, seems unveiled to faith as never before. Jesus is now realized answering the prayer—

> "Be of sin the double cure,
> Save from wrath and make me pure!"

A new sense of oneness with Christ fills the heart. The Scriptures are radiant with promises of present sanctification,—a redemption from all iniquity,—studied a thousand times, but never understood till now. Prayers for holiness are now answered, and a holy joy, a divine peace, a rest in God, and the witnessing of the Holy Spirit to the work of Christ, *for* the soul and *in* the soul, ensue.

This experience, where enjoyed, is in most cases strongly marked, as a definite step of faith, which,—whatever may be the after-growth in grace,—practically brought the soul at a definite period into new and overwhelmingly lovely practical relationships to Christ,—relationships which ought to have been entered into at conversion, but which are, alas! mostly deferred till after a long and God-dishonoring experience of wilderness failure. Sometimes, however, like the time of justification, the exact period is less defined, the blessed Word having distilled like the dew into the Lydia-like worshipping heart. But whether the experience be the work of a moment or of a year, it is the gracious operation of the Spirit, taking of the glorious things of Christ and his salvation, and showing them unto us.

Now we must inquire, What is the condition as to indwelling sin into which the soul is thus by faith brought? Is it, or is it not, an inward cleansing from *all* unrighteousness? So glorious is this revelation of Jesus as a Saviour from sin, and so complete faith's present overcoming of the world, that the consciousness cannot be trusted for a reply. We may well hesitate to accept the experience, even of our own hearts, if it be unsupported by Scripture, as well as contrary to that of others. Consciousness does not so much take note of the quiescent state of the soul, as of its activities. Whether because we do not feel the inward motions of sin, for a longer or shorter period, it is therefore purged, it is not in the range of consciousness to determine. Where *we* dare not answer, the Scripture is very definite as to what is wrought in the soul, and if the Word, fairly rendered, corresponds with our consciousness, may we not trust our convictions, as the witnessing of the Spirit. We are told that the blood "cleanseth us from *all* sin," — "from *all* unrighteousness;" that we are "made free from sin," as once we were "free from righteousness:" "free from the law of sin and death:" "light in the Lord:" and that "the truth as it is in Jesus," is the putting on "the new man which after God is created in righteousness and true holiness." The less we limit the intent of this large class of passages, and the more we cast ourselves upon Christ to have the real meaning accomplished in our souls, the better shall we understand them. Happy he who seeks prayerfully to raise his practical experience up to the level of God's word, rather than to lower God's word to the level of his own experience!

We know no one who interprets these terms in their absolute sense, as though the unconditioned holiness of God were ours. The Scripture addresses our *need* and our *consciousness*, carefully avoiding all metaphysical distinctions. My conviction is, that we do well to act on this scripture plan of not analyzing these things, but that we should simply receive them in their plain and obvious import. Care must be taken in our definitions of "sin" and "holiness." A condition necessarily imperfect in even the knowledge of what is evil, and which is capable of hourly progress in holiness, is scarcely, in the accepted meaning of words, to be therefore called sinful and unholy. We seek to use terms in the intuitive sense, comprehensible by the great mass of Christians to whom the sacred Scriptures are addressed.

God's commands are not grievous, and He does not set before his redeemed children a line of obedience through which the grace and truth that are by Jesus Christ cannot lead them. We could not say, as do some, that the injunctions of Jesus are like the law, given but to manifest the sin of believers, so as to cast them more entirely upon the atonement. Nay, my elder Brother would not leave me in so miserable a condition. He came to save His people *from* and not *in* their sins. To the flesh, or old nature, these commands are superlatively impossible, but to the Spirit-led disciple there must be far more possibility, in this dispensation, of having the testimony that we please God, than when Enoch walked with God for three hundred years.

AN AUTHOR.

Permit me to relate some simple incidents, illustrating the views here given. About three years since, I was earnestly pressed to visit a Presbyterian minister with whom I had labored in tent-preaching ten years before, He had for probably twenty years borne an eloquent and most clear testimony to justification by faith alone, both in his preaching and in his writings, issued by millions from the press on both sides of the Atlantic, and had lived a life of unusual practical devotedness to God. The Holy Spirit, however, had been leading him to a discovery of his inward corruption and deep needs, such as is referred to above.

After our first greetings, I inquired of him in substance—

"Have you, my brother, found Jesus a Saviour from this constant sinning?"

"No," was the reply; "and I feel my need of some power beyond what I have yet known."

"Do you," I asked, "believe it the will of Jesus to give you power uniformly to overcome the world?"

"I do."

"And how only can such a victory come?" I again inquired.

"By faith alone," he replied.

"Are you willing to yield yourself," I said, "to trust the Lord to work in you, *to will* as well as to do, of his good pleasure? Are you willing to trust Christ to do all that *you* have failed in?"

"I am."

I only added as I looked him full in the face, "WHEN?"

There was a severe struggle and a pause. He had not expected to be brought so soon to the test of yielding the last remains of unbelief in the power of Jesus, of giving up the very last corner of his heart to Christ; but faith triumphed as he exclaimed—

"NOW!"

Immediately he was filled with a peace in the Lord, such as he had not known before since his conversion, and found a victory over sin, and a power in preaching Christ "with the Holy Ghost sent down from heaven," such as he had never before realized. Recent intercourse with him assures me that he would not for worlds exchange his present experience of victory over sin and communion with Jesus for the former life, eminently devoted and successful in winning souls as it was.

AN EVANGELIST.

One more incident among many. In a large tent, where, in 1857–8–9, we preached to the non-church-going-masses, a young man, who came to mock, remained to pray, found Jesus, and went forth to proclaim His salvation with great success. For a while he took a charge as a Presbyterian minister, but his unusual abilities as a public speaker led him into other work, in which he travelled from Maine to California, reaching with his voice probably millions of his fellow-creatures, and with many seals to his ministry of the Word.

While earnestly laboring in an extensive field, he came to realize this need of inward holiness. After long prayer, I pressed him so earnestly to come and visit me, that, although the distance was near a hundred and fifty miles, and his engagements urgent, he dropped everything, and came. Other calls pressing upon me, our private interview was limited to about an hour. There, in the solemn searching light of God, he reviewed his life, inward and outward. The remedy for all sin and sinning was presented to him, and he saw, by the light of the Word, that it was indeed to be found in Jesus Christ. He could not, however, have faith for it. We knelt before God for the Spirit to show him the full power of Jesus, and to plead his sacrifice. His agony grew greater. He cried out, "Oh my unbelief! my unbelief!" so loudly, as to resound through the house. We could only wait upon God to show the cause of his not finding through Jesus the victory which he sought. It was then recalled to my memory that the brother had said that once he had, as he thought, cast himself upon Jesus for this victory over sin, and then immediately, to see if he were indeed able to overcome, had voluntarily placed himself in circumstances of temptation, and had failed as formerly. He wanted a *sign* before he would believe. He was now led to see that this was not faith, and that he must, as in attaining to a knowledge of remission of sins, *believe without a sign*, simply upon the word of Jesus. The last difficulty was removed, and his soul entered into a joy and communion with Jesus which he had not known since his first hours of faith in his tented birthplace.

Upon his return those in the Gospel laboring under his direction around him wondered at the heavenly change wrought in him, though they knew not the cause. A day lately spent with him, after the interval of a year, gave the additional assurance, were it needed, that this second coming to the cross was to him indeed the work of the Holy Spirit, opening the way to such victory over sin and self-abnegation as he had not before known.

Permit me, in closing this chapter, to remind you that I do not present this secret of the Lord as a doctrine to be discussed, but as a *life* to be enjoyed. I well know how little access it has to the hearts of professors, even while they lament their own backslidings, and how almost all, however they may differ in other things, unite in opposing it. I believe, however, that you are humbly and devoutly waiting upon God to open it to your understanding and heart, ready to follow whereever his truth may lead. And should I have the privilege of removing any difficulties, or of piercing the clouds to bring down a ray of hope for deliverance from this body of death, then my purpose in writing will be gained.

I know that the Holy Spirit *alone* can really unlock to your soul these treasures that are in Christ for every child of God who will hold out emptied hands to grasp them. I only add, *When Christ places them in your hand, grasp them;* hold them firmly, watchfully, feverently to the end. And *so,* having in this sphere become a partaker of the divine nature, having escaped the corruption that is in the world through lust, an entrance shall be ministered to you *abundantly* into the everlasting kingdom of our Lord and Saviour Jesus Christ.

CHAPTER VII.

IT IS THE FULFILLING OF THE LAW OF THIS DISPENSATION.

IT is remarkable how many dear Christians there are who would gladly go to the stake rather than deny their Lord, and yet who confessedly fail frequently, or even habitually, in the smaller acts of hourly obedience and consecration; and who live under a painful sense of their lack of love and obedience to God. It is remarkable, too, how many there are who appear to have given God the supreme place in their affections, who yet, —unconsciously in some cases,—retain for themselves, and for their idols, corners, hidden places as it were, in their hearts. Strange is it, too, how great the shrinking is from the thorough searching of the soul, and from yielding these last outposts after the general surrender has been made to God: —when so much of the heart has been cleansed, how great an aversion there is to the completion of the work. How many things will a man lose of the old life, how near will he voluntarily come to death, and yet at the last point refuse to "lose his life." The evil *doings* of the old or natural life may be put aside to a large extent, but the life itself, though nigh unto death, is retained by some apparently slender thread of existence. This, however, is sufficient to sustain the vitality, which anon, in a most unexpected moment, springs up again in fearful energy.

Death is a bitter thing to nature, whether it be the death of the body, or the yielding up of "the flesh" to death; the crucifixion of "the old man, that the body of sin might be destroyed;" the burial "by baptism into death;" the reckoning ourselves "dead indeed unto sin." And yet, until this is known, it is a weary and unequal struggle between the flesh and the spirit, with often most God-dishonoring results.

When the Christian, who is as yet not fully at rest in the Lord, is honest before God, and when he will come to his knees in sincerity with the heart-prayer, "Search me, O God, and see if there be any wicked way in me, and lead me in the way everlasting," there will then always be found some point of will reserved from God, some secret place of the heart not yielded, some method of acting condemned by conscience and yet allowed, or some act of faith from which the soul yet shrinks. It is most important to come into the full light of God, that this may be defined to the soul, so that instead of a general and indefinite sense of soul-weariness and separation from God, there may be the distinct consciousness of what God calls for at his hands. This is often God's first answer to the prayer for a clean heart, the light exposing the evil before the blood can cleanse. It is the purpose of our Lord's work, accepted in all its blessed provisions, that our souls should be filled with love and obedience, and that dwelling in the full sunshine of His love and favor, we should realize His love and His joy fulfilled in ourselves. It is most blessed to have a hope opened to the soul of walking thus, not sometimes in special seasons of command, but always. What the soul needs is the Way in which this can be accomplished, definitely set before it.

This result is not attained unless there be that distinct work in the heart by which the temple is emptied of *all* defiling things, and cleansed by the blood of Jesus. It can then be filled with the love of God, and consciously and definitely established in entire consecration and obedience. "Whoso keepeth His word, in him verily is the love of God perfected: *hereby* know we that we are in Him." To this agrees that word of our Lord, "He that keepeth My commandments, he it is that loveth Me."

"Oh that I *could* live thus!" exclaims some soul, weary of its wanderings and falls, footsore and despairing of ever having a heart that shall condemn it not, and leave it confidence before God,—able to enter into God's dwelling-place of love. Do you *indeed* desire it? And if some Way, clearly proven by Scripture, were set before you,—a Way possible to you just *now*,—would you at any sacrifice enter upon it?

We take it for granted that you so far trusted Jesus, as to realize that He did indeed bear your sins in His own body on the tree,—even though you do not yet find the declared result of being "dead unto sins, and alive unto righteousness,"—and that you are not now in condemnation of soul by the remembrance on your part of past "sins and iniquities," which God is pledged to "remember no more." We assume that you are not living wilfully in any known sin or open act of rebellion, and that you are groaning for that full union of soul with Christ which the Scripture sets before you.

Can I cease from sin, and dwell in love and in God?

God is our Father. He does not reap where He has not sown. He commands no impossibilities of us. He is not more unreasonable than earthly parents. No command is without the means of its fulfilment attached to it. Faith and love can meet any requirement of God, for the one brings His own power into the scene, and the other places us in God's own atmosphere of love as our dwelling-place. "For this is the love of God, that we keep His commandments, and *His commandments are not grievous.*" It would seem to be beyond question that God has provided a Way of obedience and holiness, and if you have not attained to it yet, He whose command is "Awake to righteousness, and *sin not,*" tenderly assures your heart by these words, "And this is the confidence that we have in *Him*, that if we ask anything *according to His will*, He heareth us. And if we know that he heareth us, whatsoever we ask, we know that we have the petitions we desired of Him." If it be, then, according to His declared will that we "abide in Him" and "sin not," do not hesitate to ask in confidence for such a grace, nor fail to use the means which He has provided.

It may be, however, that your theory of what is included, in this dispensation, in "the fulfilling of the law," and "in pleasing God," may be different from the definitions of Scripture. We are not called to the standard of a different dispensation from that in which our lives are to be lived. We are not called to walk by the rule of angels who "excel in strength," while we exceed all other creatures in weakness, nor yet even by the rule of the yet unfallen Adam. Neither is our standard that which will be ours in glorified bodies. "Like as a father pitieth his children, *so* the Lord pitieth them that fear Him ; for He knoweth our frame, He remembereth that we are dust." The obedience to which Christ is wooing us is not the legal obedience, a stainless perfection of knowledge and act impossible to these clouded faculties. That would indeed be an impossible and therefore grievous command. "If ye are led of the Spirit, ye are not under law." We are called to a hearty and supreme love of God, and to love our neighbour as ourselves. "Love is the fulfilling of the law." "A *new commandment* I give unto you, That ye love one another; as I have loved you, that ye also love one another." "For in Christ Jesus neither circumcision availeth anything, nor uncircumcision; but faith which worketh by love." "Love is of God: and every one that loveth is born of God, and knoweth God." "If we love one another, God dwelleth in us, and His love is perfected in us." "Jesus said unto him, Thou shalt love the Lord thy God with all thy heart, and with all thy soul, and with all thy mind. . . . Thou shalt love thy neigbour as thyself. *On these two commandments* hang all the Law and the Prophets."

Any commandment beyond the plain requirements of Christian morals is all "briefly comprehended in this saying, namely, Thou shalt love thy neighbour as thyself." It was on the occasion of our Lord's enjoining the duties of love upon His disciples that He said, "that ye may be the children of your Father which is in heaven . . . . . Be ye *therefore* perfect, even as your Father in heaven is perfect." That is, as I judge, Receive "the love of God shed abroad in our hearts by the Holy Ghost," and let that love be "made perfect" in you as children of a heavenly Father. The Holy Ghost is given to accomplish what were indeed impossible otherwise.

It would seem, then, that love is God's law and standard in this dispensation, and that whatever is not contrary to love does not now bring condemnation upon our conscience; entire obedience to the recognized guidance of God's Spirit being, of course, included in our love to God. A child's service may be accepted and acceptable, although not yet perfect. There may be many mistakes of judgment, things done through involuntary not wilful ignorance, that are not contrary to love,—on the principle that to him that knoweth to do good, and doeth it not, *to him* it is sin. And yet it is true that all our ignorance, all our failures in the best of our service, all our lack of conformity to the perfect example of Christ, need the application of "the blood of Christ, who through the eternal Spirit offered Himself without spot to God," that he might purge our conscience from the dead works of a legal obedience, to serve the living God through a divinely-implanted love. We cannot claim any perfection beyond this, that up to the furthest line of to-day's consciousness, we have the witness that we do love God and our brethren, and keep a conscience (or knowledge) void of offence.

It must, however, not be overlooked, that this

soul-attitude of obedience involves a perpetually increasing light, as well as a perpetually growing conscious conformity to God. Increasing light is the essential condition of obedience. Each day of full obedience is a day of advancing knowledge. Yesterday's standard of walk will not answer for to-day. The past twilight did not discover some defiling bone in my tent, and it did not then bring an evil conscience; but, in the clearer light of to-day, the same contact would bring condemnation. The essential thing is not perfect light or perfect knowledge, but perfect obedience to the light and knowledge already bestowed.

A just consideration of this truth would remove many difficulties from those in doubt about the possibilities of a full sanctification. It is not perfect knowledge, perfect wisdom, or perfect attainment, but simply a perfect heart—that is, a heart yielded without any reserve to God—to walk in entire obedience and perfect trust. It is that yielding ourselves to God, "*as those that are alive from the dead*," which can only be known after a practical experience of having been "buried with [Christ] by baptism into death." It is the power of resurrection life with Jesus. So far from this experience of grace being the completion of God's work, as is sometimes understood, it is but the condition of soul-health, in which a continuous, unchecked progress in the divine life is possible. It is the well-grafted and healthy tree which can grow rapidly and mature its fruit. After having presented our bodies a living sacrifice to God, then, transformed by the renewing of our mind, we are privileged to "prove what is that good, and acceptable, and perfect will of God" in all the details of daily life.

A few days since, my gentle little girl, two years old, attracted by an inkstand, innocently picked it up, poured its contents over her new white dress, and, pleased with the performance, she finished the contents over my own clothes, and then looked joyously into my face for approval. Had the child been older and wiser it would have been a transgression, and she would have needed correction; but, as I saw what was done, I could only say, "You knew no better, my little one;"—and, I thought of my Father in Heaven, and said, "Does He exact impossibilities of my ignorance, while I walk in communion with Himself and up to the light He gives me?"

"Beloved, if our heart condemn us not, then have

we confidence toward God. And whatsoever we ask we receive of Him, because we keep His commandments, and do those things that are pleasing in His sight. And *this is His commandment*, That we should believe on the name of His Son Jesus Christ, and love one another, as He gave us commandment. And he that keepeth His commandments dwelleth in Him, and He in him. And *hereby we know that He abideth in us by the Spirit which He hath given us.*" The Holy Spirit is the *direct* Witness to our spirits as to whether Christ is abiding in us and we in Him. Having this, we are satisfied. To any cavils from those who tell us that it is impossible, we may have little to answer, but our inward consciousness responds, "My Beloved is mine, and I am His!"

How can I attain to this dwelling in love and in God?

"Such a life seems impossible for *me*." So did the knowledge of the free, full, perfect forgiveness of past sins once seem. But it became true to faith.

"The placing it as a perfect love bestowed on us, rather than as a legal obedience, instead of lessening my difficulty, seems rather to increase it." So did setting forgiveness of sins as the free gift of God, and shutting you out from the least ray of hope through your own legal obedience, once seem to place salvation further off. But in like manner we are now bringing you nearer to the attainment of your soul's desires, for we are setting before you God's own way.

"But the withdrawal of all hope of accomplishing this result by dependence on my prayers, vows, and efforts, seems to take away all props and helps." Such has been our principal aim in leading sinners to the cross for remission of sins. In like manner, when your present hopes and efforts are all proved and acknowledged to be ineffectual, you will be ready to lose your own life;—the self that must be denied,—that you may find the resurrection-life of Christ in all its glorious power. You may heretofore have somewhat denied self's evil doings; now you have to deny *self* in its very centre. You may have heretofore denied some of the actings of the old life; but now you must lose that *life* itself, in order that you may experience that "whatsoever is born of God overcometh the world." You must know that the old man *is* crucified with Him, that the body of sin might be destroyed, that henceforth we should not serve sin,—an actual transaction of your soul with God,—before you can say, "I am crucified with Christ: nevertheless I live; yet not I, but Christ liveth in me: and the life which I now live in the flesh, I live by the faith of the Son of God, who loved me, and gave Himself for me."

"God is love. He that dwelleth in love dwelleth in God, and God in him . . . . As He is, so are we in this world. There is no fear in love; but perfect love casteth out fear." If the memory of all past failure, the sense of present despair and helplessness as to dwelling in love and in God, should bring you to the point of exclaiming, "'O wretched man that I am! Who shall deliver me' from this corrupting body of sin?" you are in such a place before the cross for inward cleansing, as you once were for the forgiveness of sins. Never had you been so near mercy's door as when you despaired utterly of self-merit, and of your own efforts. And now again, in that despairing of self and all its actings, of the old life and all its doings, you feel your need of the further results of the cross, for inwardly cleansing from all sin, and dwelling in love and in God, and you are just prepared to "thank God *through Jesus Christ* our

Lord," and to realize that "the law of the Spirit of life *in Christ Jesus* hath made me free from the law of sin and death, ... that the righteousness of the law might be fulfilled in us who walk not after the flesh, but after the Spirit."

What may be, in your case, the last weight to be laid aside, what the last item of self-will to be surrendered, the last thread of the old life to be severed, is known only to your own conscience, enlightened by the Spirit of God. It may be that you know of nothing in your present or future that you withhold from an entire consecration ; that you feel as though no self-will or mental reservation interfered with the yielding of the whole being as a living sacrifice laid upon God's altar. If so, and yet your soul has not entered into the full rest of God, there is but one thing remaining,—that is, to yield up your unbelief as to God's acceptance of the offering. The gift is sanctified by the altar, and what we bring to it, by touching the altar, becomes holy and acceptable to God. Our faculties and emotions are not in themselves unholy ; but have become so only by being yielded to Satan, and the *same* faculties and emotions yielded to God are made holy "instruments of righteousness to God."

"For as ye have yielded your members servants to uncleanness and to iniquity, unto iniquity; even so *now* yield your members servants to righteousness, *unto holiness* . . . . *Now* being made free from sin, and become servants to God, *ye have your fruit unto holiness*, and the end everlasting life."

Can you not, dear Christian, believe that God *now* accepts and sanctifies that which you bring, and that *through faith it is now* and *may be henceforth*, yours to dwell in love and in God?

Plainly, as once the results of faith for the remission of sins were received the very moment that faith was exercised; so now the very moment you trust Christ for realized deadness to sins and life unto righteousness, you shall find it accomplished; and the foundation having been thus laid, your faith may extend to dwelling in love and in God. The very name of "*believer*" which you take, forbids that you should defer the reception of any blessing, for grasping which you are called to believe the promises of God.

The difficulty of realizing that this perfected trust and its accompanying perfect love is now for us, is lessened by the remembrance that it is not our own natural love, the emotions proceeding from our own souls, which constitute "the love of God." "The peace of God" is not our peace of soul toward God, but His own eternal peace, in which He dwells without change, amid all the convulsions of His universe, throughout eternity; and which He sends down into the hearts of His trusting children. In like manner, "the love of God" is not born of "the will of the flesh, nor of the will of man, but of God." It is an actual divine gift, like the Holy Ghost, by which it "is shed abroad in our hearts." It is not a condition of soul into which we ourselves can gradually grow, but a divine grace bestowed on and established in the trusting heart. Since it is of God, it is perfect in its character, free and immediate in its bestowal, and through a continuing faith and obedience, permanent in its results; and since it is the soul's deepest need, NOW is God's time for its reception. I see not how any believer need despair of its full power, since *it is a gift, and it is from God,* and is to be received as a *gift,* undeserved but freely bestowed.

Once received, then follows the responsibility of keeping ourselves in the love of God. This injunction is found between the "building up yourselves on your most holy faith, praying in the Holy

Ghost," and the joy of "looking for the mercy of our Lord Jesus Christ unto eternal Life." The path of faith is always an advancing path, and yesterday's building seems to-day but as a foundation laid, so that there is the perpetual further building on the foundation once laid. "Praying in the Holy Ghost" surely authorizes prayer that God's love may be "made perfect" in us up to the utmost limit of the present capacity of these small vessels.

Oh that this gift of God in all its fulness might be received into hearts which have too long dwelt in the changing atmosphere of failing natural emotions! Listen to the tender tones of thy Beloved who speaks, and NOW says, "Rise up, my love, my fair one, and come away. For, lo, the winter is past, the rain is over and gone; the flowers appear on the earth; the time of the singing of birds is come, and the voice of the turtle is heard in our land: the fig-tree putteth forth her green figs, and the vines with the tender grape give a good smell. Arise, my love, my fair one, and come away." Oh, that thou wouldst *abandon* thyself to this love of Jesus until thou canst say, "He brought me to the banqueting-house, and his banner over me was love. Stay me with flagons, comfort me with apples; for I am sick of love." There are those whose very hearts do melt within them as they experience this divinely-begotten love of God. Such an one, a simple child-like heart, a few evenings ago, in the prayer-meeting, said, "I've had *just one drop* of the love of Jesus, and just that one drop would fill all your souls."

It is the full acceptance of this love of God, and the creation of its response by the Holy Ghost in the heart, which can alone satisfy the claims of the Heavenly Bridegroom, who tells us that his "love is strong as death: . . . . many waters cannot quench love, neither can the floods drown it; if a man would give all the substance of his house for love, it would utterly be contemned." Jesus tenderly both offers and claims such a divinely, inwrought love for us when He says, "Love Me."

Thank God, if the feeling of the need of this overcoming divine love has been created in the heart of my reader, even though it be, for the moment, nigh unto despair as to experiencing it. The creation of the felt need of a grace promised to faith in the Word, is the first step, and a great one, toward the supply of that need. Lay that need before God,—not to go away and forget it amid the myriad voices that are in the world and in the heart; but to keep it as the soul's cry continually before the throne. Can there be any doubt as to the result?

A MAN OF BUSINESS,

living in the busy whirl of large commercial operations, writes, "I have great joy in recalling the time when first those words were effectually illuminated to my soul by the Holy Spirit: '*God is love. He that dwelleth in love, dwelleth in God, and God in him.*' I could not deny that a marvellous work had been already done in my soul, in a divinely inwrought faith, which placed Christ between me and temptation, just as a screen, placed before the fire, shuts out the fire, leaving only the grateful colors of the screen before the eye. I had already known the faith which overcomes the world, inward or outward, and something, at least, of what it was to abide in Christ, with its blessed results. Yet in the thought of *dwelling* in love, and in God, and God in me, there was a vista opened before me that seemed at first to overwhelm my faith with a sense of impossibility. I dared not say, however, that any promise of God was 'not for me,' and I felt that God's hand was on me for this also. I do not remember any sudden baptism of love or of joy, but as I *continued* in prayer and faith for this gift of God, I became conscious of a marked change in my inward life. The stirrings of bitterness or contention seemed to die out. I shrunk from thinking or hearing evil of any one. There seemed an atmosphere of divine love graciously formed around and within me, so that it did not now seem so much effort or restraint to meet sudden injury or insult with love, as the simple and natural expression of the inward life of God in the soul. I remember the hour in which I became conscious that my prayer had been in a measure answered. Although I feel that all yet received from God is but a drop from the ocean of divine love,—yet it *is* that drop, and I *know* that 'God is love. And he that dwelleth in love, dwelleth in God, and God in him.' 'And hereby we know that He abideth in us, by the Spirit, which He hath given us.'"

We find, then, that—

I. Christ's command involves the truth that the believer CAN cease from conscious transgression, and dwell in love and in God.

II. It is in an unreserved abandonment of soul to Christ only, that the believer can learn HOW to dwell in love and in God.

III. Faith's NOW is the time WHEN the believer may dwell in love and in God.

We are called with Abraham, who left his *all* at God's command, to put our trust in "God, who quickeneth the dead, and calleth those things which be not as though they were;" and follow "the Father of all them that believe," who "staggered not at the promise of God through unbelief, but was strong in faith, giving glory to God; being fully persuaded that what He had promised He was able also to perform." This is the faith which brings God into the scene, negatives the verdict of experience, sight and sense,

"And cries, it shall be done."

"Let us therefore as many as be perfect, be thus minded: and if in anything ye be otherwise minded, God shall reveal even this unto you. Nevertheless whereto we have already attained, let us walk by the same rule, let us mind the same thing."

CHAPTER VIII.

IN EXALTING CHRIST IT MUST HUMBLE THE BELIEVER.

IT is manifest that every approach to God must humble him who draws near, and the nearer the place into which faith brings the believer, the more entire the withering of the flesh and self. The two evils which separate the soul from the Saviour are sin and self-righteousness; and of these two things, self-righteousness seemed to be the more effectual barrier during the days of our Lord's ministry on the earth. The self-righteous Pharisees, who wore Scripture texts up and down their garments, and who would not eat their soup till the tithe of their mint and anise had been paid, derided Him; but the publicans and sinners heard Him gladly, and were saved. We are all born Pharisees. Pharisaism is bred in our very natures; and, if we escape the upbraidings of conscience for gross sin, the natural resource of the evil of our hearts is this legal self-righteousness.

Although this evil of self-confidence is that with which the "Way of holiness through faith" is most frequently charged, and, although the confession of salvation in its full, practical, present sense might sometimes *seem* to give ground for it, yet in truth it is as effectual an antidote to pharisaical self-confidence as it is to sinning. It was precisely here, in the self-despairing confession of entire helplessness, the conviction burned into our very souls by the consciousness of inward failure, that we reached that point where a new view of the privilege of present redemption in Jesus, from all iniquity, made us burst into the exclamation, "I thank God through Jesus Christ our Lord!" It then became *all* Christ; and the soul, which could not stop to define the doctrine, joyously embraced the living Christ to receive from his hands a practical death to sins and life unto righteousness.

The *doctrine*, without the life-giving power of "Christ formed in you," is but the colorless shadow, the faint copy of the living, breathing reality. It is the possessors of this shadow who have brought reproach upon this "Way of holiness," by an imitation, which, while it presents some of the outlines, lacks the reality of the resurrection-life in Christ. We know that the devil always imitates, but never originates, and we ought not to be ignorant of his devices to throw at every point discredit on the truth of God. There seems to be a special and most marked effort by the evil one to destroy in every way the testimony of those who preach a redemption from all iniquity. We are not careful to reconcile the fleshly walk of those who evidently profess without possessing or practicing the truth of God, whether the "profession" be that of pardon of sins, or that of the faith which gives real victory over the world, the flesh, and the devil.

There is a wide difference between "professing" and "confessing." Peter professed what he would do, and he fell. Paul confessed Christ living in him, and he triumphed. In a more exact translation of the Epistles we should find the word "profess" applied in an evil sense to those who, "professing themselves to be wise, they became fools;" while we should read of Timothy that he "confessed a good confession before many witnesses." It is just here that the point now before us lies. We profess nothing of ourselves, but we *confess* that "Jesus, who delivered us from the wrath to come," now keeps us, by the power of God, practically within that kingdom which is righteousness, peace, and joy in the Holy Ghost.

So long as there is the least legal taint in our ideas as to how we were saved from just judgment for our sins, so long will the taint of self-confidence be found in the "professor of religion." But, as soon as the soul recognizes that "salvation is of the Lord," wholly of the Lord, without work or merit of our own, then at once the "profession" (implying something partly our own, which we will carry out), is changed to a "confession made unto salvation" of what Christ has freely done for us. Then, without any other trust, the soul rests on the sacrifice of Christ, and, for the first time, is thoroughly humbled before the Lord, finding it now *not* "presumption to be sure of heaven."

Those who have not the assurance of salvation, will not believe this; but, judging such a confession by their own legal thoughts of salvation, they will insist that confidence in Christ is presuming on one's own merits. Only those who have found that holiness is no longer a desperate negative strife, but a blessed positive obtainment or gift, can know how exactly parallel to the above are the thoughts of brethren who charge with presumption and self-confidence those believers who *confess* Christ as a present Saviour from sinning.

It is because with us it is ALL Christ that we are so humbled, and that we have such confidence. We find, alas! that the moment anything else intrudes into the ground of our confidence, our strength is gone. This life is one of continuous self-despair, and of continuous trust. The instant that the soul pauses to rest in anything "already attained," in that moment our feet slide. Just so far as any element of unbelief qualifies the simple, absolute trust in Christ, just so far is there transgression. Faith is the measure of holiness. But, let us always remember, that uniformly victorious faith is not an impossible faith, but, that as Jesus is the author of faith, He is, also, the finisher or perfector of faith. Here again it is ALL Jesus; and, while looking to him, we are not sent empty away. The vessel may be small, but it is filled to-day; to-morrow it will be larger, and still its utmost capacity shall be filled. Truly, here all "boasting is excluded." By what law? Of works? Nay, but by the law of faith. And yet with David we say, "*In God we boast all the day long*, and praise thy name forever." Saved from Egyptian bondage by the outstretched arm of Jehovah alone, "neither did we get the land of Canaan in possession by our own sword, nor did our own arm save us, but Thy right hand and Thine arm, and the light of Thy countenance."

Contrast the holy and happy, yet humble confidence in Jehovah, which says of the Canaan of rest, "Let us go up at once and possess it, for we are well able to overcome it," with the faithless cry, "We be not able to go up against the people, for they are stronger than we;" and we find the secret cause of the different positions of God's people. In a late church-meeting, an influential man arose and said that he loved the Lord Jesus in his weak way, but that he had sinned very much yesterday and to-day, and he expected that he should again to-morrow. The same was said by several others who had taken prominent positions among evangelical Christians.

It was not said of constitutional defects, nor of evil not yet discerned as such, but of known and conscious sins. And these frequently utter their belief that Christians necessarily commit known sins.

We could ask, How much sinning is of the nature of a necessity? If a necessity, upon whom does it reflect? Verily, such a doctrine is the very stronghold of Satan within our lines. The Lord have mercy on those who thus dishonor the work and power of Christ by saying that continuing in sin is inevitable ; and on those, too, who would not say it so broadly, but who cover up the essence of the doctrine by indefinite evasions of the issue. May we beware of this specious form of " humility," for, as the stream does not rise above its source, so their lives cannot rise above their faith, or rather faithlessness.

Such is the present experience of the church, her sins culminating in the charge against Israel, " They limited the Holy One of Israel." According to her faith she is cured, according to her unbelief the old sin-palsy returns. But we like not to hold up the unlovely picture. We would be found not so much testifying against error, as bearing a faithful witness to the truth as it is in Jesus. If we have to speak of error, it is sadly, and not for controversy. Nor does it befit one who looks back to so sad an experience of failure, and who stands from moment to moment by faith only, to judge his fellow-servants. We would rather say to them, We have found in Jesus treasures of present practical blessing, such as we had not, in our former dimness of sight, conceived of as for us in this life. "O taste and see that the Lord is good; blessed is the man that trusteth in Him. . . . . They that seek the Lord shall not want any good thing."

We dare not withhold our testimony to the power of Christ to usward, when we are conscious before God that it is given in self humiliation and to his praise. We saw a part, but now in the light of God we see full salvation in its glorious proportions. We were unholy, but by his grace we are made holy,—saved from sin to the full measure of our trust in Jesus, and filled with the comforts of the Holy Ghost. Surely it is no pharisaism to proclaim, like Paul, what God is doing for us,—no vaunting to say that we find Jesus saving us from our sins. For it is never said by any walking in this sacred light, "I am holier than thou," or "I am holy of myself," or "I can be holy if I choose." The praise for these blessings, equally with deliverance from wrath, is all given to Jesus. We hear from such, "Jesus keeps me." "I find Him to be indeed the double cure." "The blood cleanses." "I am nothing, Christ is all." "I am kept by the power of God."

Dare you, my brother, reject such a present salvation from sinning, every aspect of which is illustrated by the Word, by Christ, by the light of Calvary, by the power of the Spirit, by victory over sin, and by the genuine humility into which it introduces the believer? I am not so careful about our agreement in the doctrinal statement of this glorious privilege, as for the reality in the soul, which can only be rejected by any to their most imminent peril. The substance of the life may be held with some misapprehension of the doctrine. While I am divinely sure of the reality of the experience that "Christ liveth in me," and while, according to my small measure of capacity, I know what it is to "be filled with the Spirit," I do not feel perfect in knowledge, nor that I am able to state the doctrine in the perfect harmony of its several elements. Test all yourself by the Scriptures, *never bringing them down to the level of your experience, but raising your experience by faith to their full standard of holiness.*

If others can state these things, so as to reach the hearts of their hearers, without illustrating by personal experience, yet pardon me that in these letters I have followed the best judgment that I could gain in prayer. As the preacher's confession of Christ as his own Saviour from wrath, is the best preface to his message, so I have judged that I must witness that I have myself partaken of the fruits, in order that I may not seem to hold out an impossible privilege to those for whom I write.

And now, for the future :—I feel it most important not to set before myself any *expectation* of ever again sinning against God.* Although my past experience might seem against such a hope, and though I dare not either make vows or boast, I feel it to be most God-honoring to commit the keeping of my soul in well-doing unto God, as

* As long as David, without anxiety, trusted God without limit day by day, walking in full faith in that path appointed him, so long confidence toward God and holy communion were his. "Saul sought him every day ; but God delivered him not into his hand." But forgetting the miraculous preservation just experienced, and that he was God's appointed king, he looked at circumstances, instead of exercising that faith which is above circumstances. Then came in the evil heart of unbelief, and he " said *in his heart,* I shall now perish one day by the hand of Saul." This distrust of Him who had given him all his victories was the entrance on the shameful history of failure from which at length God restored him, a solemn warning, as once he had been an example. "Take heed, brethren, lest there be in any of you an evil heart of unbelief in departing from the living God." " For by faith ye stand "

unto a faithful Creator. *The very expectation of sinning would be its prelude*, and I must look not at sin, but at Him who saves from sinning. I can set no bounds to what God may do for the chief of sinners, now saved and kept by grace. When I have thought and asked my largest, I find that God does for me exceeding abundantly above and beyond it all. In fact, this seems to be my almost continual experience of surprise and wonder at the manifestation of God in *His* power, in *His* presence, in *His* imparted joy.

All this is accompanied by deeply increasing knowledge of self-weakness ; for the flesh does, indeed, wither at the presence of God in the soul, while yet the Spirit lives and reigns. And yet it is only by faith, and only a moment at a time, I am thus kept. The evil root is ready to spring up into bitter branches; the flesh is near me, though I walk not in it ; and the " destroyed" body of sin is ready to "revive" at any moment. Oh, hourly miracle of grace! Oh, blessed Saviour, to whom all thy children are privileged thus to cling!

CHAPTER IX.

LLUSTRATIVE CASES.

I.—A REVIVAL.

THERE is a most important rule of the dealing of God with his children embraced in the statement of the Psalmist, "He made known His ways unto Moses, His acts unto the children of Israel." Moses was on the mount, in communion with the *ways* and purposes of God, while the children of Israel trembled beneath acts which manifested the awful presence of God in their midst. Be it ours with Moses to commune with Jehovah in the knowledge of his *ways*, rather than to have our eyes so upon the world as to see his *acts* only. May we, like Abraham, the friend of God, dwell in heavenly separation, where God shall not hide from us what He is about to do!

A little church in the country had lost its pastor, and not being able to procure another, they desired a business man, who lived a few miles away, and who preached the Word, to minister among them. He found it in about the condition in which so many assemblies are found,—legal and uninstructed in some of the first principles of Scripture. Few, beside some young persons recently converted, could say with confidence that they had eternal life. One of the deacons, however, had a few months before entered with great power, into the experience of entire consecration to Christ and victory over sin. Full of faith and the Holy Ghost, his walk, and even his very appearance, were a testimony to the gospel. He was, however, comparatively untaught, and his power of expression was mostly limited to the simple, though convincing, statement of what the Lord had done for his soul. The arrangement of the meetings was of the usual kind—preaching on the Lord's day to a mixed company of saints and sinners, and on a week-day evening a prayer-meeting.

At first the gospel was preached, and strong appeals made to the unconverted, but without apparent fruit, save in two instances. Disheartened by the limited results, the preacher then, in anxiety, turned to do that which he should have done more fully at first—to ask the guidance of the Spirit, to wait for it, and to *act on it* alone.

The answer came with great distinctness in the words, "Oh, that salvation were come out of Zion! *When God bringeth back the captivity of his people*, Jacob shall rejoice, and Israel shall be glad." It was seen that full salvation should be *in* the church, before salvation could flow forth to sinners. "He made known his ways," to his weak servant, and full faith was imparted, that when the believers were experimentally sanctified, *then* the power of God in His gospel would save sinners. Close and careful instruction from the Scriptures in much prayer was from that time addressed to the believers, leading them to look away from themselves to Jesus only as the ground of the forgiveness of their sins. One by one the members dismissed their Christ-dishonoring doubts, and rejoiced in the present possession of eternal life through faith in Christ only. But they were not suffered to rest here. The foundation having been laid in Christ, they were to be *built up* in their most holy faith. The confession made by two brethren in their midst of what God had done for their souls, made the church feel that they could not take up with any rest short of the true rest of receiving *all* from God, and giving *all* to God. The aspect in which this practical sanctification was presented was chiefly as the full result of the atonement,—the privilege purchased for us by Christ, the entrance upon which thus became the most solemn obligation. The power of God in this truth reached their souls one by one, leading to full experimental union with Christ, until nearly all shared the blessing. Then it seemed as though the very windows of heaven were opened upon them in the floods of spiritual blessing and joy. The meetings were deeply quiet, and more and more solemn. The power of the Holy Ghost was seen wonderfully in the assemblies. As men are "drunk with wine," so were they "filled with the Spirit, making melody in "their hearts to the Lord ; giving thanks always."

Then with this fulness of joy came the willingness to "fill up that which is behind of the afflictions of Christ in their flesh, for His body's sake, which is the church." Then dawned in their souls *the glory of the humiliation.* They saw that the more they suffered with and for Christ, the more their place was "without the camp ;" the less that they kept to please the flesh and their natural love of position, the more they would occupy the real place of spiritual blessing. Strong cries went up to God to hide them, and to honor Christ. They renounced all desire that, as a church, they should have any honor in the community,—glad themselves to be little and unknown, if only God should be glorified in them. They asked one thing alone,—to have Christ in their midst, ruling effectually in their hearts and in their meetings, and then that from them should sound out the word of the Lord in all that region.

The answer came according to their prayer. The worldly attenders left their meetings. Their house of worship was taken from the church. Some members removed, and others were estranged. They were stripped of numbers, their house gone, and the places of loved ones were vacant. Poverty, too, pressed upon them. They were learning the lesson that God Himself was to be their only hope and joy. The lessened meetings were held in a private house, and limited to the more faithful members only, But God was there. He had now brought them to the place of need, which is always the valley of blessing. He who had "made known his ways" of first filling Zion with blessing, in faith that thence salvation should flow forth, now led their hearts to pray for sinners in prevailing power. It was not the restlessness of struggle and effort, so much as the calm confidence of faith, which, acting in the power of God, must command results,—the firm step of soul health rather than the struggle with spiritual paralysis. It was a solemn season of apparent failure of all things outwardly, and yet of the triumph of an anticipative faith. It was the Lord's way, his deep lesson in the school of God, the humiliation before the triumph.

After the more private meeting of the diminished though favored church, they were accustomed to join a much larger company on the Lord's-day evening near by, in a capacious building, erected for the joint use of all the religious denominations around. There were, however, but few meeting there who were walking even outwardly in Christian paths. Soon prayer was answered by a deepened interest in this meeting, and without any previous planning of revival services, continuous nightly meetings were called for. In these the attendance, though good, did not result in any conversions for near two weeks. The preacher who had labored in the smaller church proclaimed both God's judgments on sin, and a free, full salvation to contrite sinners. That there were no conversions closely tested the faith that seemed to be just grasping the promised results; but the trial of faith was "precious" beyond gold in God's sight. God's ways, as foreseen some months, had all been realized up to this point; praying for sinners had surely been "in the Spirit,"—and were the meetings to close without their seeing souls saved? In the smaller and select meetings the cry went up, but "Jesus answered them not a word." The answer was delayed, however, but to bring out the deeper needs of their souls. At length it seemed as though prayer must be answered, or the preacher could hardly live. Night after night, as, after the hard work of the day, he rode alone through the darkness to the meetings, his cry went up to God, and the earnestness of the appeal was at length answered by the agonizing pleading becoming the effectual message of grace.

The answer came. Dead souls heard the voice of the Son of God and were quickened into life. Large numbers responded to the call to meet after the preaching those who could answer their question, "What shall I do to be saved?" As each one entered into peace, the loudest call was sounded by their confession of Christ, and the hearts of others were reached. Persons gathered from a distance; the word of the Lord was sounded all through that neighborhood; meetings were started in other places around, and thus the faith which had through all trusted in God was honored.

Before this time, often, in preaching the gospel, the joy of seeing souls come to Christ had been mingled with the deepest sadness in the anticipation that the saved ones would, alas! too probably, soon fall into the Christ-dishonoring, faithless ways of the professors around them; but now it was a wonderful and joyous privilege to set forth Christ to the young converts, not only as bearing their sins in his own body on the tree, but as proposing to make them by that very sacrifice "dead to sins," and alive to God; to show them *in Christ* a present and practical redemption from all iniquity; and to open out to them their privilege, having left Egypt, of entering at once into Canaan, or resurrection-life and victory over all enemies.

The type or character of the faith and life of converts is wonderfully affected by the character of those who have been their spiritual parents. Where these have been themselves groping in legal twilight and spiritual paralysis, the same low type is too often reproduced. But where the preachers of the gospel have themselves had clear views of divine grace, with corresponding entire consecration to God and victory over sin, we generally see a higher faith and walk in converts. Recent intercourse with some of those saved in the revival here described, and reliable accounts from most of the remainder, give us ground to believe that the Holy Spirit who gave the victorious faith in their spiritual parents, reproduced the "like-precious faith," to a most satisfactory degree in those who made a clear confession of Christ during these services.

These special meetings presented many scenes of deep interest. A praying father saw two of his children, who were just arriving at maturity, confess Christ for the first time on the same evening. The dividing line in families between faith and unbelief was cancelled, and ties of blood were eternally cemented by union in Christ. The numbering of converts is often an evil thing; for we may rejoice over those who may go out, "that they might be made manifest that they were not all of us," and we may know as yet nothing of many whose repentance makes "joy in the presence of the angels of God." We leave all to be ascertained in "that day," when the wise, who turn many to righteousness, shall shine as the stars, and when all our crowns of rejoicing shall be laid at the Saviour's feet as the triumphs of his grace alone in us.

In a true revival, life is increased and developed by exercising its functions, instead of being merely stimulated and exhausted. Where there is excitement without development of life among Christians, the subsequent reaction places them in a condition as much below their ordinary level as the stimulus raised them above it. But in soul-health, scenes of protracted effort only develop the life within, so that increased power follows, and not reaction. It is therefore not only that sinners may be saved, that the privileges of a full soul-union with Christ are to be urged upon believers, but that, when special times of refreshing come, there may be spiritual capacity to retain the grace poured out.

The special work being ended, the little company of "faithful brethren," having done their Lord's will, returned to their more private meetings, their assembly being added to by the fellowship of some of those lately saved. Their meeting-house was restored to them, and they are now worshipping on the Lord's day in great simplicity, and holding frequent meetings through the week, in the wonderful joy and power of the Holy Ghost. He who had preached the word and taught among them was suddenly removed to a distant field of labor, but they realize the truth that "the anointing which ye have received of Him abideth in you; and ye need not that any man teach you; but as the same anointing teacheth you of all things, and is truth, and is no lie, and even as it hath taught you, ye shall abide in Him." Much as they valued the gift of a teacher, they knew that their assembly, with a public teacher or without one, was "a house of God," "the church of the living God." Though they may wait on God for another pastor, they do not for the want of one cease to know the presence and power of the Divine Teacher in their midst.

The lessons learned in this scene were,—first, the guidance of the Spirit in the assembly, pointing out the mind of God as to the present line of preaching; and, secondly, that to have a revival that can be fully owned of God, Zion must first herself be filled with salvation. We have more hope for the cause of God in seeing one intelligent soul led to this full practical sanctification in Christ, taking *all* from God, and giving *all* to Him, than in ten ordinary conversions, where the converts may probably, for want of knowledge and faith, fall into the usual ways of the correctly called "Christian *world*." For instead of a stumbling-block, the soul thus sanctified will be a power for God through a lifetime, leading many souls to like privileges.

"Oh, that the salvation of Israel were come out of Zion. When God bringeth back the captivity *of His people*, Jacob shall rejoice, and Israel shall be glad."

II.—KADESH BARNEA.

A young disciple under words of solemn warning to Christians not to be always asking God for a holiness that they could not exercise faith for, nor even hope to receive, was led to see what it was to be raised up with Christ in resurrection-life, to "sit in heavenly places in Jesus Christ," always walking in those "good works which God hath before-ordained that we should walk in them." An anxious inquiry after the meeting as to how he should attain practically to such a privilege, led to a conversation, of which the following is the substance :

"Do you desire to be *wholly* the Lord's? Are you willing to receive this full salvation at once, if God would give it to you?"

"I do indeed desire it above everything in this world," he replied.

He was told, "You must yield to God your own will, as well as all its evil actings. Not that your sacrifice is the procuring cause of God's blessings, but it removes the obstacles to their reception. *We are neither saved nor sanctified by what we give up, but by what we receive.* It is no covenant of works that is set before you, but you must not frustrate the grace of God, which can only reign in the soul through righteousness. If in anything you were regarding iniquity in your heart, God could not answer your desires for holiness. Hence, you are wholly to yield yourself to God, as one alive from the dead, and your members as instruments of righteousness. You are to realize yourself by faith as 'buried with Christ in baptism, wherein also ye are risen with Him, through the faith of the operation of God;' and this resurrection is to make you practically dead unto sins, and alive unto righteousness. Can you die to all the idols of your heart, that Christ may be formed within, reigning in resurrection-life?"

"I do not know of anything that I have not fully dedicated to God," was the reply, "but I have not the victory you speak of yet."

"But there is one thing not yet given up, and unless you part with it you can never hope for this fulness of gospel blessing."

"What is that?" he eagerly inquired.

"*You have not yielded up your unbelief!*"

He saw this last step to be taken, and powerless of himself to take it, we bowed before God for the power of the Holy Spirit. The time of our interview was necessarily limited to about twenty minutes, but God can bring a trusting soul into the land of promise directly from Egypt as easily as after forty years of faithlessness in the wilderness. Upon his knees before God, there stole over his soul, as the dew from heaven, the God-given faith by which he realized what it was to put off the old man, corrupt according to the deceitful lusts, and to put on the new man, which after God is created in righteousness and true holiness. The flesh was withered, but the spirit lived, and with a strange, humble joy, he learned the first great lesson in the way of holiness by faith in Jesus. By faith alone will he stand in this holy place. But, thank God, he *can* stand by faith in the power of the resurrection of Jesus Christ.

III.—A CITY PASTOR.

I parted with this rejoicing disciple to keep an engagement with another dear Christian, whose history may throw one more gleam of light on this highway of holiness cast up for the Lord's redeemed ones to walk in. Converted early in life, and well settled in the doctrine of justification by faith, his early joy had been chilled by some influences at a theological seminary, so that upon entering on the pastoral office, he had found a cold, professional feeling in all his work, that alarmed him. He had incurred a severe disease from laboring among the soldiers in the late Union war, which laid him by for a season, and gave him the opportunity of reviewing his past and present position before the Lord. God created in his soul deep longings for personal holiness, with a feeling of intense need for something far beyond his present life of inward failure and conscious lack of full communion with God. So deep were these convictions that after his recovery, and even during special services in the church under his care, he declined to preach, leaving the work to others.

At length, over-persuaded by those around him, he stood up to speak. In that moment, under a perfectly overwhelming sense of need, he cast himself unreservedly upon Christ, to live and act in Him ; and to his great surprise and joy, he found himself preaching the gospel with the Holy Ghost sent down from heaven, and witnessing to what God had done for his soul with a new and strange power never before known. For nearly a year he lived thus, carried above the world in the victory of faith. When he knelt for prayer, he knew not what he was about to pray for, but he felt conscious that what he should find himself asking should be done. It was the Spirit praying in him, according to the mind of God, and in the name and power of Jesus, for such things as God would bestow.

Difficulties, however, beset him. He found men "professing sanctification," and evidently walking in the flesh ; and instead of seeing that the counterfeit always presupposed a reality, he became perplexed. The privilege of such a walk of faith was not clearly set forth in the standards of the denomination in which he preached. His brethren told him it was a joy that could not last. Alas! instead of going only to the oracles of God for knowledge, and casting himself unreservedly upon Him for power and guidance, he looked to man ; he took his eye off Christ, was frightened by the waves, and his feet sank. He limited the Holy One of Israel, who had already gotten him so many victories,—and fell from the resurrection walk of victory over the world, the flesh, and the devil. He ceased to be filled with the Spirit. Several years had passed, and although considered an earnest and a successful pastor, he was now under so painful a sense of inward failure, and of want of full communion and power with God, that he was thinking of giving up his large metropolitan charge for another profession.

On the evening preceding the prayer-meeting above described, I had accepted his invitation to call upon him. Although our first interview, he freely opened his history, as related above.

"I have for months been asking God for some one to be sent to lift me out of this condition. Can *you* tell me," said he, feelingly, "how I may regain the blessed experience of joy and power of service in which I once lived?"

We opened together on Romans vii., that chapter which holds up the mirror so effectually to the experience of the failing Christian. When at last we came to Paul's fresh vision of Christ doing all that Paul had failed in,—the law of the Spirit of life in Jesus Christ setting him free from the law of sin and death,—we felt that God's hand was upon us. On our knees we besought God to restore to him the joy of His salvation, and the power of resurrection-life. The prayer was answered. He thanked God, through Jesus Christ, and left behind him,—as we trusted for ever,—"the seventh of Romans," to live henceforth in the eighth, walking not after the flesh, but in the Spirit.

A striking feature of this interview was that to almost every difficulty suggested by the remaining legality of his soul, the only reply needed was,

"*Answer as you would to the doubts of an awakened sinner.*" We found ourselves applying just such words as in his own mouth had been so often blessed to those inquiring the way of pardon—"Receive God's grace by faith alone,"—"Without or with emotion,"—"Now,"—"Step out in God's promises, and find them true,"—"It is no presumption to trust Christ for what He has promised." When delivered from his legal doubts, he confessed that while he had always preached immediate deliverance for sinners, he had indulged the subtle unbelief which argued that time, and sorrow, and certain methods of feeling, were needful to saints.

These instances of the entrance on a walk in the Spirit are selected among many as the freshest in my memory. The testimony of those who, beginning thus, have walked in God's highway of holiness for nearly half a century, could be added, were it needed. *The highway was cast up for the redeemed to walk in,* though some would seem to believe that it was only to be longingly gazed at.

A Presbyterian minister has very recently told me, that while he had not accepted either the doctrine or this "gift of righteousness," he must, in candor, say that he had often wondered at, and almost envied, the uniform elevation of piety, and the practical resurrection power in which some around him, and even in his own congregation, walked,—a power to which he was, alas! himself a stranger.

My brother, you believe in the resurrection of Jesus Christ. Have you not faith to realize practically your own resurrection? Have you consciously given up ALL to God? Is there no reserve, no corner of your heart retained for yourself,—the old hateful self, that must be denied, not in its manifestations only, but in its centre. If you have, what hinders you from being practically risen with Christ? Give up your *unbelief* in the fulness of God's present salvation!—but oh, do not turn back to the old hopeless ways of self-effort, or to a trusting in means while rejecting Christ's power.

With your sins buried in the grave whence they can have no resurrection, can you trust Christ for a present resurrection-life that knows no eclipse? Whether you sweep the streets, or ride in your carriage, you can only fulfil God's purposes of love by living and walking in Christ in heavenly places.

The believer dead with Christ should have done with the world, and find himself risen with Christ in a new life. Acceptance with God and separation from the flesh belong together. The same cross which connects me with God should be found to separate me from my old self, and not be taken as a reprieve to the flesh. Christ died that we might also die with Him, to self, to the world and to sin. The believer should not profess to enjoy the benefit of Christ's bearing his sins in His own body on the tree, and yet refuse to enter upon the experience of being "dead to sins," and of "living unto righteousness."

I do not feel at liberty to close without adding that there are many who *speak* of that which we do ourselves *know*. We are not exhorting to a path, the joy of which we are ignorant of. According to our small measure we are witnessing the results and power of our Lord's resurrection in the midst of lives of severe labor :

"There are, in this loud and stunning tide
Of human care and crime,
With whom the melodies abide
Of the everlasting chime :
Who carry music in their heart.
Through crowded streets and wrangling mart ;
Plying their daily tasks with busier feet,
Because their hearts the sacred melodies repeat."

It is not a mere ideal, nor a translation, but an intensely child-like and simple life lived out in the duties and relationships in which God places us. We are conscious of no controversies in our souls with God; and, like breathing, it becomes the habit of the soul to trust God for everything. The cross-currents are controlled, the current of the whole being sets towards God, and the soul can take up the word, "How shall we that are dead to sin live any longer therein?" We boast not of yesterday, nor make vows for to-morrow. The blood of Christ *now* cleanseth, the bread come down from heaven *now* sustains, and the faith once delivered to the saints *now* gives the victory.

IV.

One or two incidents may be better than definitions. In the summer of 1868, I met, at a large conference, a young business man, with whose variable religious experience I had been familiar for some years. The company of some who were evidently walking in an atmosphere of Christian love, and of victory over the world, to which he was a stranger, led him to feel his need of a full salvation. One evening after an address on the soul's union with Christ, he was asked the question, "Do *you* need such a life?" "I do indeed," was the reply. "And are you ready to trust Christ for a full sanctification?" was asked. "I feel that I am," he responded. Then came the searching question, "WHEN?" to which he replied, "Now!" The conversation was so simple and brief, that often as I had witnessed the far-reaching results of an immediate and full surrender of soul to Christ, I could myself hardly believe all that seemed included in those few brief responses would be realized; but soon I heard in all directions of his gospel labors, and the wondrous results. He was like a flame lighting every circle it touched; and I could name few in private life who, in the two years that have passed since that brief interview, have done more for the cause of God than this young man, although up to that time he had rather needed to be himself helped than to be called on to help others. A few days since he told me that he was living in a cloudless rest in Christ.

I recently met in a railway car, a young lady, of whose remarkable success in gospel labors among the young and educated I had known. On asking her the secret of her power, she said, that after her large Bible-class one evening, under a deep sense of need of more power in the Spirit, she asked this same young man the secret of his power, and how to obtain it. "*Just abandon your soul to Christ,*" was the brief reply. Accompanied by the Holy Ghost, it was blessed to her heart, so that before she entered her father's door she felt that she had indeed "*abandoned*" her soul and her *all*, without reserve, to trust Christ for victory over every sin, and for every blessing promised in the Scriptures to faith. Her life since seems to have been a continuous act of trust, which like breathing has become the habit of her soul. Many stars are already in her crown of rejoicing, and I doubt not many more will be found "in that day."

I like that word "*abandon.*" It expresses the soul's attitude towards Christ. This attitude may be taken up at any moment, and continued without break through a lifetime — the perfect abandonment to Christ in all his offices of mercy, cleansing, power, and guidance. It places the soul in Christ's hands, and makes Him alone responsible, if we may so speak, for all results. Our responsibility ends with the abiding: for then He Himself works in us both *to will* and to do of his good pleasure. A life of abiding is a life in which we sin not (1 John iii. 6); we bear much fruit (John xv. 5); we ask what we will, and it shall be done unto us (John xv. 7); and then when He shall appear, we shall have confidence before Him at his coming. (1 John ii. 28.)

Oh, blessed abiding in his love! Oh, blessed keeping of his commandments! How can we ever enough praise God that, in the midst of all the evil of man and of Satan, God's power can be so exercised toward his saints as to keep them abiding in the Vine, as living fruit-bearing branches!

Let none stagger at the promises of God, or fail of recognizing his grace for making them to dwell in love, and dwell in God. Oh that the simple way of faith, rendered possible by an entire abandonment of soul to Him, might become plain to all of God's children!

May our reader see by the Spirit's illumination that God's NOW is the time for availing himself by faith of the provisions made for us in our King, our Sacrifice, our Life, our Conqueror, Sanctifier, our ALL IN ALL.

www.ingramcontent.com/pod-product-compliance
Lightning Source LLC
LaVergne TN
LVHW021405110826
845150LV00007B/1798

* 9 7 8 1 4 2 5 5 1 1 9 9 9 *